MY JOURNEY

to *Jamie*
Revisited

Gail Bennett Frey

MY JOURNEY

to Jamie **Revisited**

GAIL BENNETT FRY

TATE PUBLISHING
AND ENTERPRISES, LLC

Published by Tate Publishing & Enterprises, LLC
127 E. Trade Center Terrace | Mustang, Oklahoma 73064 USA
1.888.361.9473 | www.tatepublishing.com

Tate Publishing is committed to excellence in the publishing industry. The company reflects the philosophy established by the founders, based on Psalm 68:11,
"The Lord gave the word and great was the company of those who published it."

Book design copyright © 2016 by Tate Publishing, LLC. All rights reserved.
Cover design by Jim Villaflores
Interior design by Caypeeline Casas

Published in the United States of America

ISBN: 978-1-68352-252-2
1. Religion / Spirituality
2. Family & Relationships / General
16.05.04

In Loving Memory
Greg and Brenner Wolfe
Never Forgotten. Always Loved.

REVISITED 2016

Have you ever had a conversation with someone and walked away only to have some great thought relevant to what you were talking about suddenly pop into your head? 'Man, I wish I would have told them that!', you say to yourself. You can't wait to talk to them again so you can reveal this new piece of information! Well, that is exactly how this book was born. My Journey to Jamie-Revisited is a compilation of my first two books, 'My Journey to Jamie', published in 2003 and 'Thinking Out Loud' published in 2006. I have merged what I considered the most important parts of these two books along with new thoughts to create 'My Journey to Jamie-Revisited'. Time, maturity and experiences have a way of persuading you to reflect on life with fresh eyes.

2016 is also an anniversary of sorts. I hate to use that word, anniversary, when dealing with something so difficult to talk about. But the year 2016 brings with it the twenty-five year mark of losing my beautiful fifteen year old daughter, Jamie. Twenty-five years sounds like a long time, doesn't it? Sometimes it FEELS like twenty-five HUNDRED years. But sometimes if feels like twenty-five minutes. Those are the times when our gracious Lord blesses me with a beautiful memory of my daughter. He lets me bask in her presence. I am grateful.

I want to thank you for choosing to spend time with me. **OKAY**. Find a comfortable spot. We have **a lot** to talk about.

Always,
Gail

A book. Really? **REALLY?!!** You want me to read a book? In case you've forgotten, I just lost my child and my reason for living. I barely know what day it is and you think I can focus on a book? I know you mean well and only want to help me but nobody truly knows how lost I feel because nobody, **NOBODY,** loves their child as much as I love mine. No one can even begin to know what is going through my mind—the pain, the anger, the guilt, the overwhelming loneliness and the unrelenting fatigue. So please, thank you for your thoughtfulness, but please, DON'T give me a book on how I feel.

Sound familiar? It does to me. You see, I not only wrote those words—I lived them. I do not know where **you** will be on your journey when this book reaches it's destination—your hands. If you decide to reject me at this point in time, I totally, totally understand. But please, accept this book and throw it in a drawer, throw it under the bed, throw it deep in the closet. Just don't throw it away. Maybe, just maybe, someday you will feel like talking to me. I hope so. I will be here waiting for you when you do. There is no magic pill to ease the pain you are feeling but maybe I can answer some of your many questions. Reassure you that you are not losing your mind and show you that you have permission to go on—**NOT FORGET**—but go on. I am praying for you. Hope to talk to you soon.

Always,
Gail

My Journey to Jamie

2003

It seems I provided quite a challenge for my editor and publisher when I met with them about my story. They held up the pages and said that my work was like a whole bunch of short stories. It is. They said that it appeared to be written very spontaneously, urgently, and at different times. It is. I call it "frantic writing", because that's what it is. My husband will verify that. I have bolted out of our bed many times to scribble down what was on my mind, my heart, for fear of losing it. You know-frantically. But maybe you don't know. That's what this book is about.

For some of you, my story will be like entering *The Twilight Zone*. For those of you too young to know what *The Twilight Zone* is—well, congratulations! Youth is wonderful. *The Twilight Zone* was a TV series popular in the 1960's that dealt with very strange, often eerie stories. Stories that made you think. Even frightened you. The host was this guy with a very deep, distinguishable voice. They always played very recognizable, creepy music in the background to heighten your fear. Then the host would come out and say, "Welcome to *The Twilight*

Zone". Yikes! It got your attention. Now for the younger ones in the crowd, we'll call it "Bizarro World". After I lost my beautiful teenage daughter in a car accident I took up residency in *The Twilight Zone*. Moved in right away. I lived there for many years. Only by the grace of God I am no longer there. But the time I spent there, I will never, ever forget. Inside are things I did not want to tell you. Tell anybody. But I am. I did. I have. I hope it will help you. Thank you for listening.

Gail

I magine for a moment that you "thought" you lost your child. In a grocery store, at the shopping mall, park–wherever. We've all done it. Taken our eyes off of them for only a moment and when you look back, they're gone. You call out for them and they don't answer. You begin to run and scream their name at the same time. Unthinkable thoughts start to fill your mind. The panic is like none you have ever felt before. Your heart is pounding so fast and furious that you cannot even swallow. After a few minutes (which seems like an eternity) your child comes running to you. Safe. Unharmed. Okay; now close your eyes and "imagine" you never found them. "Imagine" they never came home from school one day. "Imagine" touching their lifeless body, unable to revive them. "Imagine." A parent's worst nightmare? I cannot highlight, italicize, or underline that phrase enough to make you understand.

On August 27, 1991, the "nightmare" that we all get nauseous thinking about became reality for me. My beautiful, beautiful daughter, Jamie, was in her fourth day of High School. Fifteen and one-half years old. A Big Sophomore. She had made the Pom Pon Squad and was having the time of her life. But she always does. Jamie squeezes out every bit of energy Life has to offer. She wastes no time. She is kind and caring. She has one sibling, Shane—a big brother who has recently joined the Air Force. She has remarked that the only nice thing about being "an only child" at home is not having to share the bathroom. Other than that she doesn't like it. She misses her brother.

One of the new privileges that being a High School student offers is being able to leave Campus at lunch. I remember how great I thought that new found freedom was. Jamie relished it. A different place everyday with all of your friends. How great is that? But wait. You have to be back to school on time for your afternoon classes. No problem. On this particular Tuesday it would be a problem. Jamie and five of her friends go to Burger King for lunch. Very young drivers at the wheel. They get there just fine. It's getting back that will prove difficult. They start back to school when they are joined by another car of friends. They begin to go faster and faster. Jamie is in the back seat of her friend's vehicle. They begin to throw ice at each other between the two cars. You know. Kids being kids. They accelerate much over the speed limit. Faster, faster. Suddenly, the vehicle that Jamie is riding in loses control. The driver cannot correct it. The vehicle, carrying six young, vibrant teenagers, slams into a utility pole going 60 m.p.h. Three of the six teenagers in the car survive. Three did not. Jamie didn't come home from school that day–or ever since.

Most people will tell you that when a shocking tragedy like this happens that you will not remember the immediate aftermath. You know, from the time you are told until days or even weeks later. That all the details of what's going on will escape you. These images will not cement themselves therefore sparing you of something. That's what they told me. And for most people, this is true. They don't recall very much of the immediate aftermath. My husband doesn't. Not so for me. I remember every single person, detail, word spoken, action taken. I'm not sure why. I think for two reasons. First, I will always believe with all of my heart that when they came to my door to tell me about Jamie that God scooped me up and took me to a "protective" place that I had never been to before or ever since. I believe that God knew that my heart and mind would not survive this news. I believe He took me to a "viewing" room if you will. He left my body there and removed my heart and mind to be protected. I look back on this time and can recall it like watching a movie. I remember thinking at the time that I would be so glad when all of these people would leave my house so this horrible dream would end. It wasn't real for me. I can tell you who came to my house, where they sat, what they said, what they were wearing. Weird, huh? God was protecting me. Now; I think the second reason God has left these images so vivid in my memory is so that I could talk to you. I sometimes wonder if this is a blessing or a curse. But I know it is a blessing because sanity was always in short supply in this girl's temple so I had none to spare. See—I can still make a joke! Thank you Lord. Anyway, I just want you to know the truth. It's not always pretty but it's best that you know.

I t's a beautiful sun shiny day. I'm driving to work and singing "Amazing Grace". I love that song! I'm thinking how blessed I am and thanking God for these blessings. My life is perfect. I couldn't be happier. I have two great kids. My son, Shane, 19, has just left for Military Boot Camp two months ago. His first time away from home. Starting a career in the Air Force. I'm so happy for him and very proud too. Jamie, my daughter, 15, has just started her sophomore year in High School. She made the Pom Pon Squad and she's having the time of her life! She and I are planning her dad's 40th birthday party in 11 days. It just also happens to fall on her very first time to cheer at a football game. We're thinking of having the announcer at the football game announce it over the PA system, "Jack Fry turned 40 today!" Or maybe we'll get "Over the Hill" buttons with his picture on them. We'll think of something cool. I have a wonderful husband who, after 20 years of marriage, I'm still madly in love with. I love my job. My co-workers are my best friends. Life is great! Who could ask for anything more?

Pater Adelar,

my husband, Jack, and I so much
enjoyed meeting you last night at the
"Cenacular" group. We are so happy
to have our church share.
Thank you for sharing God's
calling in your life.

Sincerely,
Jack Berg

1-18-2019

Tuesday 8-27-91

7:10 a.m.

Jack and I are leaving for breakfast. We go to the same little coffee shop every morning where a lot of the other firefighters gather. Jamie is in her bathroom curling her bangs with a curling iron. The night before she cut her bangs herself–*just a little too short.* Now she's burned her forehead with the curling iron! Definitely going to be a bad hair day! She's laughing, telling her dad what she's done. I kiss her like I always do and tell her I love her. "Be sure and call me when you get in after school," I say. "I will," she answers back grinning at me in the mirror. I know she will. She always does.

8:45 a.m.

I'm at work. Pretty slow morning. All the kids have started back to school and college. I work in a dental office. The doctor's wife's birthday is today. She and all their kids will be in this afternoon. That will be fun.

11:40 a.m.

I'm in the drive-thru at Hardee's waiting in line to get my lunch. The fire trucks go by me on some sort of emergency. I say a prayer for them.

12:00 p.m.

I eat my lunch and I'm watering my flowers before I have to be back at work. Jack and a friend come by the house. They're doing construction work today and they've come by to cool off and rest for a few minutes.

12:35 p.m.
Jack and our friend leave.

12:40 p.m.
I'm getting ready to go back to work. The doorbell rings. I answer it and there stands the Fire Chief and another fireman who is also a good friend. They're both on duty. I know by their faces that something is very wrong. I step out onto the front porch where they are because I can no longer breathe in the house. My heart starts to pound furiously in my chest and my mind begins to race frantically. They ask me where Jack is. "OK Gail, think!" I say to myself. I now know Jack is all right or they wouldn't be asking me about him. They say they need to talk to Jack and me both.

"OK Gail, **THINK, THINK!**" I know if something was wrong with Shane it would be the Military standing here instead of them. It must be my mom or dad. They live just down the street from me. "Something's happened to my mom or dad, right?" I say. "No, Gail," was their answer. We **REALLY** need to find Jack they keep saying. "OK, something's happened to my brother or sister, right?" I ask. "No, Gail," is their reply again. They begin to press closer in towards me and I tell them my dog will bite them if they come too close. Breathing has become extremely difficult and I don't want to continue this conversation anymore. Go away! They say there's been an accident. They want to know if Jamie wore blue shorts and a white shirt to school today.

The night before I had watched Jamie iron her blue shorts and white shirt. She told me she didn't really mind ironing that much. She wanted to look nice. Again they ask where Jack is and I cry out "Not Jamie?! Dear Lord, please, please not Jamie?!" I wait and pray for their reply to be the same as before, "No, Gail." But it doesn't come. Only silence. I cry out, "Does she need me?" "No, Gail," is their reply. I begin to run down the street as fast as I can all the while praying, pleading with God to let her be all right even though I know in my heart that she is gone. I burst into my parent's home and collapse on their floor. My mother screams at me, "Gail, what's wrong?" "Oh, Mama, they want to tell me something bad about Jamie and I won't let them."

12:45 p.m.
The world as I knew it had ended.

T he next three days before Jamie's funeral service are filled with images that I have kept in my heart. Images that I can vividly *see* in "my mind's eye". I can *see* firemen taking turns standing guard in front of my house. One in particular, I remember, would not sit down or take any nourishment during his watch. Firemen are a special breed of people. The best. Jamie was so proud her dad was a fireman. I *see* all the big fire trucks with their flashing lights illuminating against the dark sky as they led her procession to the cemetery. Yes, just like the movie, *Backdraft*, which of course was her favorite movie. I *see* people I haven't seen in a long time. Friends. Relatives. All coming to tell Jamie one last goodbye. I *see* a large church overflowing with people; so they stand in the hallways, Sunday School rooms, wherever they can. *Thank you all so much for being there.* I *see* a young teenage boy stepping out into the aisle to give me a beautiful flower as I am leaving the church. I kiss him on the cheek. I *see* a big, long car with many doors that I must get into. I know it will take me to a place I don't want to go. I wish I didn't have to. I *see* a town, a community, weeping for three precious lives that will be missed forever. I come home from the cemetery and wonder when I will finally wake up so this nightmare will end. Little did I know that I was about to go on a journey that I believe will last a lifetime.

Please Lord, hold onto my hand very tight.

Revisited 2016

S till holding on. **Ever So Tightly.**

After Jamie's accident everything changed. What used to be right was now wrong. What used to be easy was now hard. Feelings, emotions, attitudes, ambitions, relationships. You name it—nothing was the same anymore. Life was a struggle to say the least. Simple questions like, "How many children do you have?" asked by innocent people left me speechless and crazy. "Oh, Gail, go ahead and say two." Oh, what if they ask me how old they are, where do they go to school? Do I say Jamie is 15 or how old she would be today? Oh my gosh, how much can I tell this person? How much do I *want* to tell this person? Will I start to cry again? Right here? Probably. I'm exhausted. Why did I leave the house? Get the picture? Daily routines were not routine anymore. The word routine completely slipped from my vocabulary.

Jamie's accident was in August and Thanksgiving was the *first* holiday I had to encounter. I would later find out there would be a lot of *firsts*. Jack was on duty at the fire station and Shane was still away so I was left to go by myself to Thanksgiving dinner with all of the

family. I somehow got through it. A week or ‗
I was at my parent's house and my mother started to talk about all the Christmas plans. "Great!" I thought to myself sarcastically. Just what I wanted to hear. I couldn't care less about tomorrow and here she was talking about Christmas. She was talking about the upcoming family gatherings. "Yeah, yeah, right," I think to myself. She looks at me and says something about how she hoped I would be better company than I was at Thanksgiving. "What did she say?" I thought. You have got to be kidding! I had come to the dinner like I was supposed to. I sat at the table. I swallowed the food. I had done what was expected of me. I went through the motions. I was indignant! I was furious that she would even think that I was less than gracious and proceeded to tell her so! My mom and dad both listened to my outrage with tears running down their faces. These were the two people who had cloaked Jack and me with a shield of protection after Jamie's accident. They had opened up their home to everyone so Jack and I could have our privacy. There were no limits as to what they would and did do for us and here I was screaming at them! Well, when I finally spit out all my vile (sorry), my mother in a very quiet voice said, "But Gail, what you don't understand is that when we lost Jamie, we lost you too." "**NOW** what was she talking about?" I thought. It didn't take me long to learn that what she had said was so very, very true. The Gail that loved to smile and laugh and be with people

more than anything in the world had gone. Here was a Gail that had become bitter, angry and cold. A Gail that would run away from people that she knew and loved just to avoid conversation or contact. I had become someone I didn't know or like. I mourned for Jamie and I grieved for Gail; for I had lost them both.

Shortly after Jamie's accident I went to work on her room. Months before she had asked me to redecorate her room. I love to interior decorate. She said I could take down her posters, change paint color, wallpaper, whatever I wanted to do. She was fast becoming a young woman and wanted her room to reflect this. "Just surprise me," she said. My daughter trusted me. What a compliment! I never got around to doing it. You know; I thought I had time. Needless to say this is something that will always bother me but in my heart I know Jamie is not mad at me. After the accident this became my mission. A source of energy. Jamie's room had to be perfect for her! So I set out to do just that. Nothing of hers could leave this room. I allowed myself to bring in new items that I thought would please her, but I totally dismissed the idea of removing any of her precious possessions. Everything had to be perfect. You know—museum like quality. Soon after I had finished, my sister-in-law came over and went into Jamie's room. I couldn't wait to show it to her! She and Jamie were very close. She tearfully looked at her room and said, "It looks like Jamie just stepped out for a moment. That she'll be right back." "Well, there! What a compliment!" I thought to myself. I had done it! I had accomplished just what I had set out to do! I had taken my decorating project to her bathroom as well. My sister-in-law could not bear it and left. So now I had two rooms in my house that were Off Limits–Viewing Only Please. I had immobilized myself without even realizing it. I then set out to *change* every other room in the house. We even added on a den and a dining room. Where Jamie's room had to be frozen in time–every other room had to be "stripped". I did everything I could do to change that house short of burning it down. A year and a half later we sold the house and left. The house that was once "Home" to us had lost it's character. There was no more laughter or loud music. The phone didn't ring off the wall anymore. The familiar smell of cologne, deodorant and hair spray didn't linger in the hallway. The sweet wonderful words, "Hey Mom!" were only an echo now. Our house was dead, or so I thought. So hence I started down the road of what has turned out to be a costly, exhausting, but truly valuable learning experience for me. At this writing we have moved 7 times in about 10 years. Each move I carried with me every molecule of everything Jamie owned. For those of you who haven't moved in a while, believe me, it's still as hard as you remember it to be! Let me tell you, Jamie saved everything. I mean everything! Girls do that.

On one particular move, 6 years after Jamie's accident, I did something I thought I would never do. I went into "Jamie's closet" to get her clothes for yet another transfer and my heart was overwhelmed with sadness. The clothes that I cherished so much and had taken such pride in carrying with me from place to place had changed. The clothes that had once given me such joy had begun to deteriorate. I could no longer smell "her smell" in them. The styles were outdated. Elastic had become stiff and hard. The glue that had once held the soles of her shoes had dried up and let go. Jamie would not wear these now. She was 21, not 15. The time had come for me to let these precious articles go and I knew it. Where they once had brought me joy, they now brought sadness. I gathered them up except for a few precious things that I could not part with and took them to a Homeless Shelter. I knew Jamie would be proud of me. As hard as it was for me to do this, I knew for me the time had arrived for this step to take place. I had finally learned that no one can ever take Jamie from me because she is in my heart, my mind, my being. In the past, I had always worried so much about Jamie's "things". I worried someone would break in and steal them or that a fire would take them from me. When I was finally able to let go of them "willingly" I knew it was the right thing to do. For someone else that "time" could have been right after the loss of their child, or two years later or ten years later or never at all. This is your decision and your decision only.

Ultimately you are the one who will have to live with it, not someone else. Whatever decision you come to over this, please be assured that your child is okay with it too.

One last thing I've been thinking about. In our society I have seen people pay literally thousands of dollars to own personal articles of some celebrity or person considered of stature. These people will then wear and display these articles they've purchased with great pride and happiness; and we find absolutely nothing odd about this. But a person who exhibits this same behavior with personal articles of their actual "loved ones" whom they personally know and care about, is somehow thought of as "odd". Society deems this act as being "unhealthy". Whoa!! I certainly think we have our values mixed up. I proudly wear Jamie's clothes and a necklace with her name on it. Go for it!

What I'm about to say next will sound too heart-breakingly familiar to some and to others a pretty good reason for my sanity level to be checked. Anyway, I figure there's safety in numbers and I know there are many, many out there just like me.

There is this woman I know. After suddenly losing her daughter she felt she couldn't stay in their home any longer. The pain was just too intense. So she started moving. She moved and she moved and she moved. That's right– 4 times she moved in a 24 month period. One place 30 days, another 5 months, another 8 months. Each time thinking she would start to feel "at home". It didn't work. No matter where she went it wasn't right. This woman goes to the grocery store and picks up a bag of potato chips. She looks at the "freshness date" on the front of the package. The date on it is the date of her daughter's death. She immediately puts them back on the shelf. No way can this come into her house with this date on it, much less eat them. When this woman goes shopping, anything, I mean anything that has her daughter's name on it she has to buy. It doesn't matter whether it's a hair barrette or a key chain, she has to get it. But by far the saddest of all is when this woman sees a young girl that even so slightly resembles her daughter she rushes to get closer to her. The urgency overwhelms her. She has to see her face, look into her eyes, all the while hoping and praying that maybe, just maybe, someone has made a terrible, terrible mistake and her daughter really isn't gone after all. In the back of her mind reality rears it's ugly head but it will not stop her. She cannot help herself. She presses on. To look at this woman you would think her perfectly normal. There is nothing unusually different about her. Nothing the naked eye can detect. But what you don't see; is that within this woman lies a broken heart, a shattered dream. And on her back she carries a trunk heavily laden with memories; for this is all she has left of her child.

Pretty bizarre stuff, huh? Before Jamie's accident I'm sure I would have agreed with you. Now I call it pretty normal. You see, **I am that woman.** Over the years I have discovered that I am not alone on this pattern of thinking. I have met one dear mother who cannot let go of a box of Fig Newtons because her son had eaten out of this box and they were his favorite. They are in her freezer. She lives with the fear that someone might accidentally throw them away, not knowing their great value. I too have a box of Pop Tarts with this high priority. Then there is the "Make Believe". In one of my many moves I had to move into a two story house because

Jamie and I always wanted one. I would stand at the bottom of the stairs and look up onto the second floor landing. I would pretend that Jamie was leaning over the railing, laughing and talking to me. Another mother would run into her house when the boy next door would play basketball. She would close her eyes and pretend that it was her son bouncing the ball outside just like he used to. I could go on and on and on but I think you get the picture. For those of you who can say "Been there, Done that" my heart goes out to you. Please know that you are not alone or crazy. You are very, very injured.

To this day, many years after Jamie's accident, when I see a mother with her daughter (especially a teenage daughter or young woman) my heart breaks a little bit. I begin to wonder if this mother knows how lucky she is. I'm not jealous. Well, maybe just a little bit. I hate to admit that about myself. The thing is, I know how very, very blessed I am to have had Jamie with me here on this earth for fifteen years. But that also makes me very much aware of how much I have missed. The Proms. The Graduations. The Wedding. The Grandchildren. The Girl Talk. That is what makes me sad. But I promise you, I would rather have had the 15 years with Jamie and the heartache I feel now than to never have had her at all. She is worth every bit of pain I feel now because the mere thought of her and her smile floods my heart with joy. This will sustain me. God be with you.

We live in a society where we believe in the idea that everything "can" or "has to be" fixed. I think this way of thinking is probably one of the reasons that the terribly irritating phrases like "the healing process" and "closure" comes from. We all yearn for some kind of beginning, middle and end to things. Summation. This is simply not true for the loss of a child. What does closure mean anyway? I will never, ever stop loving or missing Jamie. What exactly do people want me to close? Do they want me to stop talking about her or what? Sorry, that's not going to happen. Jamie is, was, and will always be my beautiful daughter. No one can ever take that away from me. I have to learn to carry her with me in other ways since I have temporarily lost the ability to have her physical presence with me. God has blessed me and taught me ways to keep her spirit and her joy with me. As for "the healing process"–Don't even get me started there! Too late–my pen has already started to fly across the paper!

April 20,1999—The Columbine High School shootings. Fifteen people shot to death. Fourteen are children.

These children have not even been removed from the crime scene and already the media and counselors and "professionals" are talking about beginning "the healing process". The speed and flagrancy of which this phrase is used is nothing short of insulting and insensitive to me. It's very obvious to me that they have not lost a child.

I believe that the first year after losing a child is filled with "Stupor Shock". Your mind and body go on what I call "automatic pilot". You may get up and go to work, pay the bills, buy groceries, cut the lawn–all done on "automatic pilot". Your body is there but your heart, spirit, and mind are somewhere else. Kind of like when you're driving somewhere in your car and your mind is so preoccupied that when you get to your destination you don't even remember driving there. You can't remember going through the intersections. Were all the lights green? That's what I'm talking about. I think it's sort of a built-in protective device to keep you from losing your mind. Kind of like being knocked unconscious in an accident. Your body is being hurt, but you can't feel it while it is happening to you or remember it because of an unconscious state. Anyway, then one day you sort of "wake up" and realize to your horror that what has happened really is true. **NOW** you start to grieve all the while everyone else around you is thinking that surely that "ol healing process" has done it's work by now and begin to wonder what's going on with you. Please don't misunderstand me. I'm not trying to be bitter. I'm past bitter. I'm just trying to tell you the way it is.

I live in a suburb just outside of Oklahoma City. On the first anniversary of the Oklahoma City Murrah Federal Building bombing, reporters, news media, and most people in general were shocked to find out that the victims of the bombing tragedy had not been successfully "healed". They were absolutely stymied! They were simply at a loss for words. It just couldn't be true! It's as if they wanted to say, "Hey guys; it's been a year now. Haven't you heard of that 'healing process'? Well, we've been talking about it since an hour after the bomb went off! Surely you've had enough time to heal by now!" Yes, that's what it feels like. I very recently heard a national news person after an interview with a parent that had lost a child say, "I guess some wounds never heal." Thank You.

The Healing Process

I understand that challenging this long standing, widespread belief is nothing less than daunting. I am here to say that I believe grief is a side effect of loss. As long as the loss exists so does the side effect-grief. So let's accept that and learn more about how to live with it or manage it–grief management. We all acknowledge depression, anxiety, and phobias as very real things, which they are. We treat these and the people affected with respect, as well we should. These same people have learned how to control and manage their handicap to go on and lead productive lives. It's something that they live with, fight, and try to manage every day of their lives–also like grief. They know it's not going to go away so they learn to manage it. I feel that grief is the same way. Grief is something I will live with from now on, and I accept that. Some days are better than others just like any of the other people we have mentioned. I am certainly not going to use it as an excuse to quit living as some people might think. I just want it acknowledged for what it really is and not swept "Under the Rug" with a phrase like "the healing process". One of the greatest compliments that I believe can be given is from people who have met Jack and me after Jamie's accident and been stunned to learn that we had lost a child. Their reactions have been, "I never would have thought that. You seem so happy." We have learned how to manage our grief. We hurt as bad as the day her accident happened but God has given us the strength to manage.

I believe there is a special language that exists among parents who have lost children. As far as I know it's never been documented but I can assure you that it exists. I would be very hard pressed to give it a name. You see, it's not just words. It's also silence, stares, touches, mannerisms. We use a lot of gut wrenching, "You know?" and probably the most repeated phrase is "I still can't believe it". There is no school or textbook for this language. The only way to scholar this language is to meet the one glaring pre-requisite–lose a child. In my opinion, there is no higher fee. While writing this book I became discouraged many times because my heart was overflowing with emotion that I wanted to put into words but somehow could not seem to. I was worried that maybe I wouldn't have enough to say. Then the Lord graciously revealed to me 1 Cor. 14:6-12 where Paul tells us that it is better to speak five words that people can understand than volumes that they cannot understand.

Just before the third anniversary date of Jamie's accident I received a card in the mail from a dear couple who had lost their teenage son only months before we lost Jamie. This is a quote in it's entirety from the card: "Just wanted ya'll to know you are in our hearts as the third anniversary nears. Unbelievable!" Love, Connie and Lucian. Two sentences! The last sentence being only one word, yet it said more to me than an encyclopedia could! You see, we spoke the same language.

I have also learned that ordinary words begin to take on whole new meanings. You become very sensitive to every word people say. Everything suddenly becomes magnified. One mother who lost her toddler daughter took great offense when people used the word "lost" when referring to her daughter. She said that she had taken very good care of her child and using that word made her feel like she had not been a careful parent. That her child had gotten literally "lost," somehow contributing to her death. This word upset her very much. Another mother could not stand to hear the word "closure" because it made her relive the closing of her son's casket. That's what drove her crazy. And I think I'm safe in saying that the words "healing process" drives us **ALL** crazy! For me, the words die, died, dead, or killed cannot be used in the same sentence with my daughter's name in it. I know what happened to her, but to hear those words together with her name crushes me. I have to use the word "lost" or "Jamie's accident". I think anyone that knows me very well at all has pretty much figured this out. And you **CAN** figure it out if you will just listen to how the parent talks.

To this day, ten years later, when someone says Jamie's name and connects those words with it, part of me starts slipping. I don't even hear what they are saying after that. I'm too busy trying to find my escape route. I know I have to get out of there, and quickly. I know for friends and family I must make you feel like you are entering a verbal "mine field" just to hold a conversation with us. I truly don't want you to feel like this. But if you really want to make a difference, just listen to us. Or better yet, just come right out and ask if you're not sure. Honesty is still the best policy.

I remember before Jamie's accident I had known a few people that had lost children. I remember feeling so awkward and anxious about maybe saying the wrong thing. I was so afraid to talk about **MY** children for fear of hurting this parent. I understand that feeling of uneasiness; of not knowing what to say or whether to say anything at all. Believe me, I now know that the parent you're talking to is just as afraid as you are. Every parent is different about what they can handle sharing about their child and with whom they feel comfortable sharing them with. Some find it extremely difficult to talk about their child while others gush. Please do not confuse this reluctance to talk as some sort of loss of interest. It is absolutely not true. Everyone is different in what they can share with people. It has nothing to do with how much they love or miss their child. Every personality is different, but their pain is the same. **So,** if you haven't figured it out by now, I'm a gusher. For me, I knew from the beginning that I was never going to stop talking about Jamie. The difference now, is that when I talk about Jamie; recall events, statements she made, things she did; I know you will have heard them many times before. But you see, I won't be having any *new* ones to tell you. This will not stop me. I too, am still a proud mother. My family is wonderful about sharing Jamie. Thanks guys!

Guilt is an odd thing. You would think it would only loom in the hearts and minds of wrongdoers therefore accelerating the conscience to correct their errors. Not always the case. Obviously so or we wouldn't have crime, would we? No, the kind of guilt I'm going to talk about is the kind that exists within you even when you know rationally in your mind that you are not responsible for it.

I somehow, no matter how hard I tried, felt guilty for Jamie's accident. Weird, huh? Was I there? No. Could I have somehow prevented it? No. Then why do I feel this way? I don't know. I just know I do. The only answers I can come up with are two. They are #1– The devil is the master of confusion; and #2– I'm the mom. Answer #2 is the one I can identify with the most. "I'm the Mom." You see, in the past I had always been able to "fix" things for her, no matter what her problem. You know what I'm talking about, Mom things. That was my job and I loved it! Now I was overcome with this sense that I had somehow failed her. I hadn't protected her. What had I done wrong? I'm the fixer of all things! She depends on me! I am responsible for her. This somehow has to be my fault, because you see, I'm the Mom. That's how I felt and still have to fight off to this day. Just a few days after Jamie's accident my sister-in-law told me something that I will never forget. She said, "Gail, you were the most over protective mother I have ever known. You thought of things to warn your kids about that never even crossed my mind. And then you let Jamie do something as simple as go to school." Wow. I know in my heart and mind that I am not responsible for her accident but sometimes I actually have to "thought process" this out to finally go on.

Now, answer #1– As I said, the devil is truly the master of confusion. I think he invented it. As long as you stay confused it makes you afraid. Afraid to take one step forward for fear it will be the wrong one. He sends out all sorts of deceptive messages into your mind. His goal is to paralyze you. Just like he does with the irrational guilt trips. Please be aware of this and learn to recognize it for what it is– deception. Only God can help you sort things out. Please let Him in.

The Serenity Prayer

God grant me the serenity to accept the things I cannot change The courage to change the things I can and the wisdom to know the difference.

Revisited 2016

I still feel guilt in many ways and over many things—some rational and some irrational. Although, I must say, I'm getting better and quicker at recognizing the irrational guilt thoughts and disposing of them quickly. But I am thankful for the pangs of guilt because without them I would have no conscience. And when you lose your conscience, you lose your way and are in great danger of losing your soul. Please be careful.

D ear Friend,

Please do not tell me this horrible accident was God's will. I'm not buying it. If you somehow think it makes me feel better, you are very, very wrong. The God I know and have put my faith and trust in is an all loving, caring, compassionate God. I don't believe that God *willed* Jamie to lose her life violently at the age of 15 years old. I do believe that God could have altered or even averted this horrible tragedy to never have even occurred. But for reasons unknown to me, God chose not to intervene. I do believe that God allows things to happen after we, as human beings, make choices in our lives. But there is a huge difference between it being God's will and God allowing things to happen. I have no answers to satisfy the nagging questions of "why, why, why?" but I am not going to blame it on God. I would be lying if I said I never asked God, "Why Jamie?" I do. That is the human characteristic in all of us. But if you believe that every tragedy is always "God's will", then what is prayer all about? God tells us to pray and ask for the desires of our heart, a situation to be altered, a person to be healed, all kinds of things. He tells us to bring everything to Him in prayer, no matter how big or small. If everything was so *concrete, unchangeable, willed;* then there wouldn't be any need for prayer. I certainly do not have any answers nor do I possess the celestial intellect needed to understand them if I did. I just know that I will put my faith and trust in the knowledge that God is in control even when I don't understand what's going on.

Gail

Revisited 2016

God's will. Okay. I will never know God's plan for Jamie's life even if she would have lived to be 100 years old. **SO**, was the accident God's will for Jamie's life? I don't know. "But she was so young and innocent. She had her whole life ahead of her," you say. **I know**. I have seen cancer, Alzheimer's, depression, abuse and neglect dismantle human beings one piece at a time. It is horrifying to watch. These were all good people— people we would label as non-deserving of such suffering. And then I am reminded that certainly the least deserving person of all was Jesus Christ, God's only son.

God's will was to have a perfect world for us all. Adam and Eve submitting to sin changed the course for mankind. God gives us free will and the consequences of that gift is ours to bear. I strongly believe in the power of prayer and God's holy intervention. I wish I could give you some satisfying, comforting words to deal with this subject that would ease your aching heart. My Sunday School teacher and dear friend, Jim Patterson, sums it up best for me. He says, "If I understood everything that God did or allowed, then that would make God only as smart as me. Pretty sure that's not the case."

This question of whether it was God's will or not will eat you alive if you let it. It is a Rubik's Cube that will only bring frustration and despair. After years of torment I have finally put this subject to rest. I pray you can too.

> "For my thoughts are not your thoughts, neither are your ways my ways," declares the Lord. "As the heavens are higher than the earth, so are my ways higher than your ways and my thoughts than your thoughts."
>
> Isaiah 55:8,9

I'm sorry that I cannot give you much information about the effect the death of a sibling has on a person. They seem extremely reluctant to talk about it, but I believe the effect to be extremely profound. In some cases, life altering. I believe they experience feelings of extreme guilt about being alive even though they know they are not responsible for their sibling's death. You and I both know that rational thinking goes out the window when it comes to matters of the heart. For most of them it is also the first time they have seen their parents weak and not in control. I cannot imagine their horror and fear. Shane and Jamie were extremely close. He was her big brother who she adored and he took delight in watching out for her. I know that Shane grieves greatly over Jamie. He doesn't say much but I know that he loves her and misses her very much. He doesn't have to put it into words. I can just tell. You see, without his realizing it, he too can interpret and exhibit that special language we talked about earlier. I know his sense of loss runs that deep. He has come a long, long way and I am ashamed to say without much help from me. I am so proud of him and his accomplishments. He has overcome many hardships. God has answered many prayers on behalf and for this young man. He has many special gifts. The following is something I wrote soon after Jamie's accident but never gave to Shane until now. Thank you for letting me indulge.

Dear Shane,

Please forgive me if I have neglected or hurt you in any way over the loss of our Jamie. You see, I have never lost a child before and am very new to this kind of shocking, raw, agonizing grief that lasts a lifetime. Please know that my agony and grief would run just as deep for you and I would be asking her for forgiveness. You and Jamie are my joy. I love you.

Love,
Mom

Several years later, on my 45th birthday, I received a card from my son, Shane.

It read:

Happy Birthday Mom! After all these years you still look great! Any woman who raised me should look like Hell by now! (Courtesy of Carlton Cards)

Then Shane wrote:

Mom, you've been great to me all these years. Even when I, and life, hasn't always been that great to you.

Love,
Shane

Thank you dear Shane, for this confirmation that I so badly needed. Thank you.

Revisited 2016

My Dear Shane,

Hi sweetheart! You are now a grown man and father and I am so proud of you. I see the unconditional and limitless love that you have for your children. **NOW** you can fully understand the kind of love I have always had for you—unconditional and limitless. And like most everything in life, until you experience something for yourself or walk in another's shoes, you cannot truly appreciate the gravity of one's words or feelings. I love you, dear son. I love you.

Mom

T hank you Luke! Bless his heart, he has no idea how much he has helped me. All these thousands of years later his words were exactly what I needed to hear! After Jamie's accident I started searching the Bible and other books of reference for answers to the ten million questions that were running through my mind. I have never, ever doubted that Jamie was in Heaven. My problem was the nagging question as to "when" you go to Heaven. Do you go immediately upon death or are you in some kind of "holding pattern" until Judgement Day? Well, I can tell you the "holding pattern" theory drove me crazy to say the least. I wanted to know exactly where she was, right now, without question. I thought I knew, but I guess I wanted to see it "in writing" so to speak. Well, I did find it in writing! Luke 23:42-43. This is the conversation between Jesus and one of the thieves while they were on the crosses. Verse 42 is the thief talking to Jesus: "Jesus, remember me when you come into your kingdom." Jesus answered him, **"I TELL YOU THE TRUTH, TODAY YOU WILL BE WITH ME IN PARADISE."**

Yea!! Luke was the only disciple or any other author in the Bible to record these words between Jesus and the thief. These are very, very important words to me. Jesus did not say in ten days you will be with me in paradise or in five years or ten thousand years you will be with me in paradise. He said **TODAY**! He didn't say that we were going to be put in layaway until Judgement Day and then we would be in paradise. Jesus paid the price for us **IN FULL**– that day! As a mother this information was invaluable to me. I know that Jamie is in Heaven **NOW** and that she is very busy doing all kinds of work for God.

Revisited 2016

To this day, almost 25 years later, Luke's words continue to give me enormous strength. I say once again, "Thank you Luke! Thank you!"

Gail

While trying to prepare myself to talk to you about the next four subjects something I had never realized before dawned on me. An epiphany of sorts! I want to talk to you about anger, sadness, fear and loyalty. It is my opinion that not one of these feelings can exist without the other to some extent. You know how in the Bible where it says so and so beget so and so and so and so beget so and so? Well, I believe that sadness begets anger and loyalty begets fear. It may not always go in that order but they all definitely connect in some way. At different times in our lives one of these four feelings may hold a bigger space than the others but the domino effect is definitely there. I'm telling this to inform you. To make you aware of what's going on. Sometimes that helps.

Anger

Anger. If we could harness the energy that anger produces we would never have to drill another oil well! Anger slipped into my life very quietly and very quickly pretending to be my new best friend. It became my constant companion. This kind of anger was different than any kind I had ever felt before. It woke up in the morning with me, stayed all day long and then went to bed with me at night. It gave me tremendous physical energy or it put me into such a state of fatigue I couldn't move. No in between. Looking back on it now I envision myself behaving like a small child does, walking off the playground angrily shaking his fists. I was mad at the world so "I wasn't going to play anymore!" I hadn't "gotten my way" so off the playground of Life I stormed! I'll show them! I mean that. Literally. I quit my job. I quit my friends. I quit my family. I quit life. I stood on the "sidelines of life" for many years just daring someone to put me back into the game. Unless you have lost a child, I find it difficult to believe that you can even begin to imagine the involuntary thoughts that race through your mind. Hopefully by reading this far you have gotten a small glimpse. Anyway, I was convinced that no one-I mean no one-had ever known the kind of pain I felt. I truly believed that no one could love their child as much as I did Jamie, so how could anyone possibly know how I felt? I was very, very wrong.

Very soon after Jamie's accident Jack and I began receiving all kinds of literature from organizations concerning bereavement and loss. They encouraged us to attend their meetings and become a part of their group. "Who are these people?" I thought. "I don't know you and I don't want to know you! So leave me alone! We have nothing in common!" **NOW**, I'm a firm believer in timing and tact. I am sure these are very good and helpful organizations, but please, let me come up for air first! Please remember that until just a very short time ago these people were "Mom and Dad" and now they're something called "bereaved parents". They will fight it tooth and toenail and have every right to do so. Nobody "wants" to be a bereaved parent. So please just be there for them. Don't try to "fix" them.

I believe that anger by far is the most dangerous of the four above mentioned feelings. It can take your life and leave you breathing. Please be very careful with this one. It wears many disguises. Don't let it destroy you. I want to tell you something that Shane told his dad and me just days after Jamie's accident. He said he could just envision God and the devil talking. The devil telling God he could have Jamie because he would get three in return; meaning Jack, Shane and myself. He very nearly did.

Loyalty

Loyalty. You know that ferocious, lioness like protective device that we have built into us concerning our children? The one that gives you the ability to run into a burning building after them or take a bullet for them without a second thought? Defend them at all costs, no matter what? Well, that loyalty, that feeling, doesn't go away when they do. A parent will always want to protect their child and now suddenly after they are gone you don't know how to do this. Believe me, the feeling is as strong as ever and always will be. You are left with this tremendous frustration that defies explanation.

One of the strongest and most dangerous deceptions I believe you will encounter is the idea that if you try to live life again, you are somehow being disloyal to your child. Remember, I used the word deception-falsehood. The devil will take advantage of your frustration, weakness, pain and fatigue and lull you into the belief that living, smiling, loving is wrong. The devil wants to convince you that if you give up your life to anger, sadness, fear of living, that you are "showing the world" how loyal you are to your child by in effect giving up your own life. He is so convincing at it. Believe me, I was convinced of this for a very long time. It's so, so untrue. But you will have to figure this out for yourself. I promise you, your child will be so happy and proud of you when you do. Jamie's time may have been brief here on this earth but she continues to teach me the "value" of life, oddly enough, including my own. Remember the smile you once saw on your child's face? It would look so beautiful on yours. Wear it with pride.

Fear

Fear is a feeling that exists whether we recognize it as that or not. I have many fears. I think one of the biggest fears that a parent like me has is the fear that people will forget their child. Friends, loved ones, please don't let that happen. Include this child in any way you can, whether it be reliving stories of happy times with them or displaying their picture. Please, please don't leave them out. This is like putting a dagger in the heart of this parent. Believe me, they will notice if their child's picture is not up on the wall with all the other grandchildren, nieces, nephews, whoever. Don't leave them out.

Then there's your memory. It suddenly becomes your greatest ally or your worst enemy. I would hear a song on the radio and think to myself, "Did Jamie like that song or not? I remember discussing it with her but now I can't quite remember what she said…" You curse yourself for not having listened to her every word closer. You grasp for any fragment of dialogue that you can squeak out! Anything! It's now of monumental importance! So you *drag* the river bottom of your mind hoping, praying to dislodge some remnant of any memory of any kind about your child. You pray it will float to the surface of your consciousness and give you some sort of security. Lord, please, please help me to remember! This is an example of a regular occurrence in my mind. After Jamie's accident everything in life was and still is put into two categories-before her accident and after. It is now as common a record of time to me as a.m. and p.m. is to most people. Every event, every element of life is now processed this way. That's how I think-in those terms. I don't think there is anything bad or damaging about this. That's just the way it is for me. And I suspect for a lot of people.

Fear for me is living longer without Jamie than living with her. But when I let that fear grip my heart God reminds me that I am never without her. I love the verse Heb. 11:1. "Now faith is being sure of what we hope for and certain of what we do not see." I believe.

Sadness

Sadness is washing your child's clothes knowing it will be for the last time. Cleaving onto some to keep their "smell" alive as long as you possibly can. Searching for strands of long, blonde hair anywhere you can find them-laundry, furniture, car, carpet. Sadness is seeing your child's classmates grow up, get married, have children. Sadness is the empty chair at the kitchen table. Sadness is the silence that pounds so loudly in your ears.

Sadness is outliving your child. What can I say about sadness? I could write hundreds of examples that would break your heart, but you want to know the bottom line? I am sad because I miss her. I just plain miss her.

S ometimes when I am driving down the road (I'll probably get my license revoked for telling you this!) I feel like my head is so filled with thoughts that I don't know if my neck can support my head any longer. The weight of all that *thought traffic* (that's what I call it) is just too heavy for me to keep my head suspended. That's pretty scary! I wish I could even slow it down sometimes, you know, put it in neutral and just let it idle for a while. Can you tell I grew up with a brother and a dad who loved cars?! Anyway, when rush hour hits my brain—**WATCH OUT!** That's usually when the devil tries to slip in wearing a policeman's uniform. You know–he's only there to direct traffic; help you out. Yeah, Right! **BE VERY CAREFUL!** The road he wants to direct you to is called The Point of No Return, Desperation Road, or Hopeless Hill. He has many different names for them and changes them often to confuse you.

After Jamie's accident, I think I went down every road in the devil's neighborhood. You are so physically and mentally tired that these somehow look like the right direction to go. Please dear friend, take the detour. Go out of your way to avoid these places. I know it is hard. But for some of us, a stop on one of these streets may prove fatal. I promise you, your child does not want that for you. Your child is not in this neighborhood. You will not find him or her there. Please seek God. He knows the right direction and will get you safely home. You are always in my prayers.

P.S. When you need to—Take the bus. Let someone else do the driving. God Bless You.

I have learned that there are places in your mind that you "must not" visit. You simply cannot go there. They are very dangerous if you do. This place for me was letting my mind "visit" the actual car accident. You know; what actually took place. These would be my thoughts. *Did Jamie see the utility pole coming her direction? Was she afraid? What was she thinking? Did she feel pain? Did she cry out for me?* Dear God—I cannot go there in my mind. I may not make it back. Seriously. I cannot go there. The devil taunts me but I literally have to physically get up and go. Please do not visit these places. They serve no useful purpose and can change nothing. I know that Jamie is with God and was from the moment they struck the pole but believe me, the devil will tell you otherwise. It will destroy you. Know your limitations and guard them. God Bless You.

THE RULE BOOK—You know the one I'm talking about. The one everyone else seems to have read but you. The one that tells you how long you should grieve, when to go back to work, what to do with your child's possessions, how to act towards others. The one that usually makes everyone else feel better but you, and usually told by someone who has never lost a child. Yes, **THAT'S** the one I'm talking about. Okay, this is my Rule Book. Rule #1— There are no rules! End of book. Each person has to do what they can do when they are capable of doing it. Things are not black and white anymore—right or wrong—this or that. Suddenly there is all this "gray matter".

Daily life, feelings and emotions have suddenly become unpredictable. Each new day brings with it challenges you could never have imagined before. Your despair and grief consume any reserve of energy that you might have stored up.

There are so many changes this parent has been forced to accept, all the while their heart and spirit are broken. Please don't make it more difficult by forcing guidelines, mile markers and time tables upon them. Please be patient and kind to them. They need your love and encouragement now—not your rules and speculation. In their own time they will find their way back. Thank you.

Very recently there was a statistical study published on parents who had lost a child to death. This study revealed that 85% of married couples who lose a child will divorce. Shocked? Not me. In fact, I'm really surprised it's not higher. I have heard it said that when a person loses a child it *hollows* them out. I think this is very true. What that parent allows to enter into this *hollow* space can be pretty scary stuff. A lot of times the anger and bitterness sets in so quickly that drugs, alcohol, infidelity, substance abuse are used to numb the pain. Then there's the silence between the parents. Neither one able to express what he or she is feeling–both afraid of hurting the other. It's kind of like the blind leading the blind. So up goes the wall. There is usually blame, guilt, and always confusion that leads to separation. The rest of the scenario is pretty evident. I expect that my husband, Jack, will be awarded some huge medal when he gets to Heaven for the incredible tolerance he exhibited here on earth towards me. This man, who was hurting every bit as bad as me, chose to put me and my pain first in his life. I am ashamed to say; I let him do it. As I said earlier, we moved many, many times after Jamie's accident. Most people believed it was because we were making profit off the sale of these homes. Not so. If they only knew the financial peril I put us in. We have been in some houses as little as thirty days and I would insist that we move, and move quickly. So you don't wait for the right price to sell– you just sell. He would build me the "house of my dreams" only to find out that it had become a nightmare. I now know that for me I will probably never feel at "home" anywhere. I don't believe I have a "root" system anymore. But that's okay. At least now I realize that and hopefully can better understand and discipline myself.

Now, when I said earlier that I had quit my job, my friends, my family and life I wasn't kidding or exaggerating. One of the many responsibilities that I totally abandoned was preparing meals or even going to the grocery store. We had absolutely no food in our house of any kind for many, many years. Literally none. No milk, no bread, cereal, soda, snacks, nothing. Dog food was the only food allowed in. We ate every single meal out. Every single one. Breakfast, lunch, dinner. Sounds impossible, doesn't it? But it can be done, very expensively I might add. I can remember actually going to bed hungry on several occasions because I was too tired to go out for something to eat. Thank goodness, every other night, Jack got a decent meal at the fire station.

WHY this man didn't divorce me, I have no idea. Yes, I do—by the grace of God. Jack is a much more godly person than I could ever hope to be. He accepts the strength that God offers him and uses it to take care of me. I admire him; I love him; and most of all I thank him for loving me in spite of all the additional pain I have caused him. I am very, very blessed. So, now I'm here to tell you, your marriage will not survive if you don't have God in your life. I'm not making an idle prediction. I'm stating a fact. Please, I pray that you won't let yourself become another statistic like the ones in that study. You and your child deserve better.

P.S. You can now come to my house and actually have a soda or a bowl of cereal. I never knew Frosted Flakes could taste so good!

There's something I've been thinking about for a long time. I really didn't have to address it–put it into context–until now. It seems to some that I may have difficulty keeping the past and the present separated. Well, I can't separate them. I won't. Before you get out the straight jacket and the Valium, let me try and explain something to you. It will be very hard to put into words, but I will do my best and pray that God will do the rest.

Jamie is as much my daughter today as she was the day that she left this earth. She is and always will be a part of my being; my existence. The experience of knowing her makes me part of who I am today. The present. I think about her everyday, many times, just like I do my son, Shane. I value her opinion on things. She left me with a lot of opinions. We girls do that. Now, God has never once told me that I had to "give up" Jamie. Never. Not once. I may have buried her little body, but He has taught me how to keep her spirit alive and for that I am eternally grateful. I think about and talk about all the wonderful times with Jamie. I love when people say her name and recall memories that they have of her. I have many close friends that let me share Jamie with them and I love you guys so much for that. They truly make me feel like they are comfortable talking about Jamie and that I'm not a crazy person. They're curious. Not nosy. Big Difference. They are not afraid of me. They love me and I know it. I am **SO** blessed to have these people in my life.

I know that Jamie is not physically here with me, and **NO,** I don't hear voices in the background. I know that I cannot physically bring her back, but I can certainly keep her spirit alive. She was a part of this world. She made contributions to life. She made a difference and she can continue to do so—if we let her. Don't let their spirit and significance die. This is very important. I believe that God has shown me how to do this. It keeps me sane and keeps my heart from completely breaking. It may not be the right way for everyone to deal with loss, but it works for me and many people like me. Please respect that, even if you can't understand it. Now, please stay with me. I promise I will tie everything together in just a moment. Thanks.

The newspaper said I was a "survivor". At least that's what it read in the obituary. "Jamie is *survived* by her parents"…and so on and so on. You know how it goes. The thing is, I don't *feel* like a *survivor*. But that's what they say that I am. So, how do I learn to do this thing (survive) that once seemed so simple to do? As simple as breathing? Well, it is not easy and cannot, I repeat cannot, be done without God's help. Jamie is, and always will be a part of my past, my present, and certainly, most certainly…my future. In my future I will live eternally with her in Heaven. So why can't we let each "transition" overlap with the other? It doesn't have to be harmful and can be done with the grace of God. He has done this for me and I am so thankful for that. So now you say, "This must be a tough balancing act." Well, I quite agree with you. But for me, it is well worth the effort. You see, this is how I "survive".

P.S. Remember, there is a big difference between surviving and existing. By the grace of God I am surviving, not just existing. Thank you Lord for teaching me how.

In Matt. 5:4, Jesus is quoted saying, "Blessed are they that mourn, for they shall be comforted." I believe that. He has done this for me many times. Comforted. Given me gifts of comfort. Please look at this verse a little closer and do not take it out of context or give it another meaning, as I believe so many have. Jesus said, "for they shall be comforted." He did NOT say "for they shall be healed." Huge difference. I believe God will give us gifts of comfort to sustain us. I believe He knows we need these gifts desperately to go on. Without knowing it at the time, God gave me one of these *gifts* three days before Jamie's accident.

On the Saturday before her Tuesday accident Jamie gave me a note she had written to me at school. She gave it to me, I read it, hugged her and thanked her for it. I folded it up and put it into my jeans pocket. I had her note that she had written to me in my pocket, on my person, when they came and told me the news about Jamie. Here is the note, the *gift*, that I so badly needed then and from now on. I have read it so many times over the years that I could repeat it verbatim to you.

Mom, Hello! I'm in 3rd hour Mr. Pennington's Algebra class. I just got done taking a test. I wanted to write you this and tell you you're the best mom in the world. I appreciate everything you do for me. I just wanted to make sure you knew that and you know that I love you very much! You're the best, #1 mom in the world; even though we do argue a lot, (and it's most of the time my fault!) We always have fun sometimes too! Just getting to talk to you, I enjoy that a whole lot. I'm sorry for all the money I take from you too. As soon as I can I will get a job and I'll start paying for most of the things I need. You are very special to me and I don't know where or what I'd be without you. I love you!

> *Your daughter,*
> *Jamie Lin Fry*

Wow.

A month or so after her accident I gained enough courage, yes courage, to change the sheets on her bed. She had always done this herself. Between the mattress and box springs I found a book– her diary. I reluctantly opened it and the first words you see are "For My Eyes Only! This means you Mom!" When I saw this I laughed. I could just hear her saying that! I didn't betray her confidences or privacy too much but something caught my eye as I was flipping through it. In her own handwriting I saw these words: "Jamie Lin Fry Loves (she drew a heart for the word loves) Jesus Christ." Boy! What a gift! Did I need that and just at that time!

Over the years, just when God knows my spirit is running low–close to empty–He gives me a gift of comfort. He sustains me. He's given me wonderful dreams of Jamie where I get to be her Mom again, even if it's only for a short while. I wake up and recall them vividly. They refresh my soul. He gives me gifts of memory that just pop into my head. Things I thought I had lost. I believe these gifts are there for the taking but only if we will accept them. They are there for all of us, not just me. Just as uniquely as God made each one of our children, so is the manner in which He will sustain us. As we all know by now, "loss" is not a "one size fits all" garment. God is the tailor in our "Custom Fit Life". Please accept these gifts God has for you. You'll be amazed at just how many there are all around you, just waiting to be opened.

MERRY CHRISTMAS.

Revisited 2016

This is very difficult for me to talk about. Excruciating to recount. I will do my best.

The realization or reality of time stopped promptly for me the moment I was told of Jamie's death. Time was no longer of consequence to me since I had lost all use of it nor considered it of value anymore. Not so with organ donation. Organ donation RUNS on the consequence of time. Healthy human organs for donation have to be harvested in a very short period after death takes place for them to remain viable. Jamie had VERY healthy organs. She was only 15 years old—on the Pom Pon Squad—in great shape—Remember? Within an hour of being told that my healthy, beautiful daughter had been in an auto accident and consequently lost her life, I was being asked if I would be willing to donate her organs. At the time, this is how it *felt* to me. "We're sorry Gail, but Jamie has just been killed in a car crash and oh, by the way, can we cut her open and take out her healthy organs?" In reality these were very kind and professional people just doing a very difficult job. Please keep in mind that until 30 minutes ago my life was just as normal as yours. My mind was being told every parent's worst nightmare and I was fading fast. My little girl has been hurt and now they want to hurt her more?! I **HAVE** to protect her! I remember flying into a rage, screaming **"Do not touch my daughter! Leave her alone! Do not touch her!"** My heart and my mind could not take any more punishment. **"Please God,"** I prayed. "Let this be a mistake."

Twenty-five years later, I am an organ donor. It is on my driver's license. I believe that Jamie would have gladly donated any and all of her organs to save another person's life. I will also be the first to say that if Jamie could have been kept alive through an organ donation I would have done anything for that organ donor's family. Sadly, this was not to be. Now, I am not telling you all of this to promote organ donation. Absolutely not. I just want you to know that if you are one day faced with this decision on behalf of a loved one, and you decide to donate, then you have given some family a second chance at life. A wonderful gift. But if you decide not to donate, for whatever your reason, you are **not** a monster. I am not a monster. You just make the best decision you can at the time. It is not possible to make the wrong choice because there is no wrong choice. I pray this decision will never befall you. God be with you.

Gail

I don't know if I will tell you this part of my story. I haven't decided yet. It is extremely personal, as well as painful. I don't know if it will help you. I have bared my soul. If I tell you, I know the next time you see me you will no longer see "just me". You will be able to look right into my heart and mind. I don't know if I can do that. It scares me. I will have to pray about it.

Going to see Jamie for the first time after her accident is the most terrified I have ever been in my entire life. There are no words to describe my fear. The last image that I had of Jamie was seeing her laughing and kissing me goodbye as she left for school. Now, I was standing in a funeral home about to enter a room where I did not know what to expect. I had carefully given someone Jamie's favorite Pom Pom uniform, clean underwear and socks and her Pom shoes. She always looked so beautiful in it. I was terrified. Jamie and I had discussed funerals before. We had both jokingly, and not so jokingly, said that we did not want anyone to see us dead. We wanted our caskets closed the whole time. We joked that we weren't going to spend our whole lives putting on makeup and fixing our hair everyday to have someone screw it up at the end! We laughed but we were also serious. I remembered what she had said. Now, I was standing in a doorway, physically shaking with fear, terrified to take a step forward. Jamie wasn't hurt very bad at all on the outside. I have told no one this. I only allowed a few close family members to see her. One of the last things I could do for her as her mother was to protect her wishes and *Come Hell or High Water* I was going to do it. We stood guard over her. Shane had a leather jacket that Jamie always loved. He put it over Jamie's legs to always keep her warm. Jamie had not ordered her High School class ring yet and loved to wear mine. I left it with her.

I used to stand over Jamie's bed while she slept and would watch her tummy go up and down with each breath, just to make sure she was still breathing. I cannot begin to describe my sadness now.

Wow. Just a few days before my story was literally about to "go to print" something "bleeped" on my radar screen (my brain) that I just couldn't let go unsaid. Of course it came to me in the middle of the night!! (2 a.m. to be exact). A new word. A very ordinary word that somehow all these years had escaped me. It must have been hovering somewhere beneath my "radar level" and my conscious state of mind wasn't able to pick it up. Very clever.

You want to hear what it is? **COPE.** Let me say it another way. I have learned to cope; I am coping. Isn't it great?! I'm so excited to "discover" this word! It's not offensive. It's not angry. It's not submissive. It doesn't have a defeatist attitude. It's not saying "I'm healed" or "have found closure" (Yuk!!). It says I'm suffering, but by the grace of God I can make it. Don't you just love it?! I do. It's amazing how such a tiny little word can mean so much- kind of like the word love does. Thank you Lord.

Well, it's now pre-dawn and I'm very tired. But some-day we'll have to talk more about this great "find". But right now, I'm going back to bed. I think I can sleep a little better now though. I pray you can too. Goodnite and God Bless.

I hope the experiences that I have told you will serve as some sort of map for you. I've tried to be your emotional meteorologist of sorts. I can forewarn you of the storms and turbulence ahead but I cannot make them go away. You will have to walk this road yourself. Some of you have already logged many miles down this stormy, frightening road; while some are just now packing the car. Sadly, some of you don't even know you're going to make the trip yet. Please know that as frightening as this is that you **CAN** and **MUST** depend on God. He will ultimately be the only one who will always be there with outstretched hand no matter how many times you fall. He doesn't keep score. He's a Good Guy. His patience is limitless. I know first hand because I have tested it many, many times. I would have given up on me a long time ago; but not God. I used to tell my kids, "There is nothing in this world that you could ever do that would ever make me stop loving you. Nothing." God has proven that to me as His child many, many times.

In closing, I want to thank you for listening to me. It has been good to talk to you. Through talking to you I have come to recognize something of great significance. I have now realized that the day Jamie left I put myself in prison. I sentenced myself to Life in Prison. I have now served ten years of my sentence. And you know what? I think I'm going to let myself out on parole. Oh, I've still got a life sentence but I think by the grace of God I can make it on the "outside" now. I can just hear Jamie cheering! I pray that you don't impose upon yourself as heavy a prison sentence as I did. It feels good to see the sun again. God bless you always.

Gail

D ear Friend,

Thank you for reading my story. I wish now that I could tell you that what you have just read is only fiction. That all of the characters and events portrayed have nothing to do with real life or real people. That any similarity to real events or real people are purely coincidental. You know; the kind of message they put at the end of a movie during the credits releasing them from any liability. You know what I'm talking about. Well, this is different. Every word I have told you is the truth. Real people. Real events. Real pain.

As I'm sure you have all guessed by now, I am not a writer. Never have been. Never wanted to be. Never will be. Why God placed this burden on my heart to write my story down will always be a mystery to me. I fought him ferociously about it for many years. Writing this down was very, very difficult for me to do and gave me no pleasure or self-satisfaction at all. If at any time God would have released me from this responsibility, I would have gladly and gratefully walked away. He did not. I said all of that to say this: In the course of getting my story to print I was asked to get additional stories (experiences) from parents like me who had lost a child to death. As I suspected, their reactions were pretty much like me. They didn't want to. They couldn't. It was just too hard. To write down horrific details about how you lost your child and to invade the privacy of your pain is just too much to ask. I totally, totally understand. How, when, and other details of how a parent loses a child may have been different from Jamie's story, but the end result is the same. **LOSS.** So, the following pages are something of a gift I wanted to give to these parents. A Love Letter to their child. To many this may seem a little "crazy" but to those of you who feel that way please be grateful that you can't understand this gift. You are very, very lucky. Again, always keep in mind; There but by the grace of God, go I. I will begin with my letter to Jamie. Thank you again, dear friend, for listening to all of us.

Gail

Dear Jamie,

Hi Baby! I wanted to drop you a line and let you know how we are doing. **JAMIE.** I love your name. I miss saying it a hundred times a day. **JAMIE. JAMIE. JAMIE.** It's so nice to hear it out loud. I hope you liked it as much as I do. You never said and I forgot to ask.

Yesterday was your 26th birthday. For the 11th time this special day that once brought such joy and happiness now brings pain, sorrow and longing. But Jamie, I so much celebrate the fact; the blessing; that God gave you to me at all. It just wasn't for long enough. But I now know that "Forever" would have been the only acceptable amount of time for me.

Our 15 years together were so wonderful. You taught me so much. I know—it's supposed to be the other way around. The parent teaches the child— Right? Well, you remember how "goofy" I can be sometimes. I think about our conversations a lot. I really **WAS** listening. I don't know if I ever told you, but I always so admired your optimistic view on life. You get that from your

Dad. You know me—I still see the glass "half empty" and fully believe in "Murphy's Law". I'm trying to be better though. The trouble is, that since you left everything is much harder. The world is not so pretty to me anymore. But I promise you, I will keep trying and never give up. I owe that to you. It took me a long time to figure that out.

Shane is 30 years old now! Can you believe it?! You kids are making me old! **HA! HA!** He is still very good looking and still in the Air Force. He's working his way back up, Jamie. We all fell a very long, long, hard way when you left. Keep praying for him; for all of us.

Your Dad is still working as hard as ever. He turned 50 last year. Weird, huh? He's still as handsome as ever too. Remember when we were planning his 40th birthday party for him? It was 11 days after the accident. We didn't have a party then or ever since. I'm sorry. I know you would have wanted me to. It's just hard.

Cookie is 13 years old now (91 in dog years). We've tried hard to take good care of her. I know how much she means to you. She has been a huge source of comfort for me; especially the nights that your Dad is gone to the Fire Station. Thank you for picking her to be your dog. She's a gem.

As for me, well what can I say? The past 10 years have been sort of a blur for me. We lost Grandpa 8 years ago to cancer. But you already knew that, didn't you? I am trying hard to go on but it's very difficult because I miss you so much. I know you are fine and in the best place ever, but it doesn't make me miss you any less. God has been very good to me and kept my "shell" from cracking completely. The blessed assurance that God has given me that I will be with you again keeps me going. I will try my best to do what God would have me to do. I will make it. I have to.

There have been so many things I wish you could have been here to help me with. I depended upon you a lot. You and Grandpa were my "cheerleaders" in Life. He always had the ability to calm me down and reassure me that no matter what "everything would be all right"– even if it wasn't going to be. And you–You gave me the self confidence that I am so low in. You gave me courage and the "grit" to know that it is better to have tried and failed than to never have tried at all. Truly I have learned that the person who has never failed or made mistakes has never done anything either. Now that you both have left, I often feel very weak and vulnerable. But I am going to try hard to be a "cheerleader" in Life for someone-anyone- everyone. I know how very important it is to "be there", "give encouragement" to people. It truly can mean the difference between life and death for some of us.

It's weird getting old without you. I look at my face in the mirror and see time marching across it (Sometimes **STOMPING!**). And my hair! My hair is so gray you wouldn't believe it! Don't worry. I'm keeping it colored. I told your Dad the other day, "I spend twice as long getting ready in the mornings to look half as good!" I will keep trying though as long as hair color and cosmetic companies stay in business! I don't mean to sound vain. I just want you and Shane to be proud of "their Mom". You know what I mean.

Jamie, there are so many things that I miss about you. I miss your laugh and your smile so much! I miss hearing you say, **"Yeah, Right!"** and **"Whatever."** I miss dancing to the latest music in your room. You and Lauren laughing at me! I miss our shopping trips. Laughing in the dressing room when we tried on ridiculous things. I miss knowing that if I have food stuck in my teeth you will be sure to tell me. I miss sharing clothes–mostly yours! I miss you "rescuing" me from unpleasant social situations. (Remember?) I miss your advice on hair, makeup, life–everything. I miss going to the movies together. I miss telling secrets. I miss your honesty. I miss your love. I miss my daughter. I miss my best friend. I miss you.

Okay–I better stop right now and close this letter or I won't be able to finish. It has been 10 years, 6 months, 17 days since I have touched your silky blonde hair, looked into your twinkling green eyes, or hugged your neck. But you know how excited you get when you know you're going on a vacation or a trip and you dream about it before you actually go? The excitement that engulfs you? Well, that's what I dream about now. When we're all together again. Until then I will carry you with me in my heart, my mind, my spirit.

Jamie, you will always be my beautiful daughter and no person, no passage of time, no worldly event can ever, ever take that away from me. I love you Jamie, with all of my heart.

Love,
Mom

At this writing, I am sorry to say that I have not received any letters back from parents who wanted to participate. I guess it was just *too hard*.

In Conclusion:

For God so loved the world, that He gave his only begotten Son, that whosoever believeth in him should not perish, but have everlasting life.

John 3:16

Jamie Believed.

THANK YOU Lord.

Thinking Out Loud

2006

Jamie,

I have to talk to you! Right now. It can't wait until I see you again. Something is weighing on my heart and mind so heavy that we have to talk **now.** I have tried desperately to dismiss it but the thought has already entered the gates of my mind and will not go away.

I was riding in the car with your dad the other day; looking out the window, thinking about you, as I so often do; when a voice inside my head, barely audible but resoundingly clear, made an announcement. It stopped me cold. It said, "Jamie died." I can barely write down the words much less say them out loud. In the thirteen years that you have been gone I would **never, ever** allow myself to think or say those words. And now, here was this **intruder** pushing it's way into my thoughts saying the very words that I could not. And you know what? I think it was you.

All these years I led myself to believe that the acknowledgement of your death was somehow saying that you ceased to exist. That is so, so **not** true. Your spirit, your love I carry with me daily. Your smile is on my face. You could never cease to exist. It has taken me a long time to realize that the "D" word cannot hurt me or you. I don't think I will ever be able to say the "D" word with your name connected to it outside the confines of my brain, but I'm not afraid of it anymore.

I suppose I will always feel like I've been "gut punched" when someone says to me that you died or even worse—that you were killed. But that's because I love you so much and I will always want to protect you; even when I can't. That will never change.

Wow! Am I glad to get that off my chest. Thank you, sweetheart, for listening to me. I knew you would understand.

All my love forever.
Mom

"Now faith is being sure of what we hope for and certain of what we do not see" (Hebrews 11:1). That is probably my favorite verse in the Bible. I repeat it to myself many times each day. It calms me. You want to know why? Because I **believe** it. But it wasn't always like that.

Now, I have always believed in God and been a Christian pretty much all of my life. But in late summer of 1991 my beautiful 15 year old daughter, Jamie, was in a violent car accident that took her life. That is when I lost my faith, my heart and my way. I wandered aimlessly for many years after that. I waited anxiously for my heart to explode. As I tossed and turned, God never left my side. He waited patiently for me to return to Him. And when I did, He never scolded me, chastised me or was critical of me in any way. He just said, "Welcome back. I've missed you so much. I never let you out of my sight and caught you every time you fell. I love you." I know He does. Remember, God gave **His** child so that I could be with mine.

Tucked inside these pages is my heart—still broken but beating loudly and stronger. I hope the news of my journey will help you. God bless you always.

Gail

I lost a friend today and I don't even know his name. He is a small, elderly man with beautiful snow white hair and moustache. He wears glasses that magnifies his kind, caring eyes. His tan face always wore a smile that you could tell was never forced. He walks with a cane or a walker; depending on his needs of the day. I would see him everyday at a little coffee shop that we both found refuge in. He was always by himself as was I; both seeking human contact. The food is OK but the company is 5 star. He called me by my name. I wish I knew his. He spoke often of his children and grandchildren that he cared so deeply for. I enjoyed our conversations.

I have just left the coffee shop and been told the sad news of his death by the waiter who works there. He not knowing his name either; known only by descriptive, kind words. I will miss this man. That is probably the highest compliment I feel can be given to another human being—to be missed. You see, this man made a difference and he **chose** to do so. Over the years I have come to realize that life is going to *happen* whether we choose to participate in it or not. This man chose to participate, even with hardships. His presence in my life, however brief, made an indelible impression on me. He made me smile. He made me "think" about the things you and I are discussing now. On my way home from the coffee shop I was wondering whether he had gotten the chance to meet Jamie, my daughter, yet. I hope so.

When it is time for me to leave this earth, if someone can feel about me like I do about this man, then I will be happy. I will have made a difference. If someone can say, "Do you remember that girl who came into the coffee shop that always had a smile on her face? I sure do miss her." I will be thrilled. I will have done my job.

I have decided that maybe names aren't that important. People are.

Every night before I go to bed I have a routine I go through. Most of us do. I wash my face and brush my teeth. I then get down on my knees beside my bed and pray. I **cannot** go to bed until I actually complete all of these things. Sounds like a good thing, right? You would think. The only problem is that by the time I get around to doing these nightly rituals, I am exhausted. I know I should go to bed earlier, but hey, that's a whole other subject!

Anyway...one night as I was kneeling down and *praying* I realized I really wasn't praying at all. I wasn't really *talking* to God; I was just leaving Him a recorded message. One I knew He had heard a million times before from me. You know the one. The standardized prayer we have memorized and could say in our sleep; which I sometimes did. When I really started to give this some thought it put me in mind of a TV or radio program that has been pre-recorded to be aired later. Then when they do air the program, they tell you intermittently **not** to call in. They tell you that the program had been recorded earlier; that it is **not a live broadcast**.

Don't call in because nobody is there! Well, that's pretty much what I was doing to God. If God had wanted to talk to me during my prayer He wouldn't have been able to. You see, I wasn't giving Him the courtesy of a live broadcast. I was too tired. I felt ashamed. Can you imagine God's disappointment as He rushes to answer your call only to find out He's reached your recording; not the live broadcast?

I then began to wonder if God has Caller ID. I suspect He does; and you know what? God would have every right to "screen" His calls but He doesn't. He picks up even when He knows it may just be another recording from me; or you. I fear sometimes we may become like a telemarketer; only calling when we need something or "want to sell an idea" to God.

Please don't misunderstand what I'm trying to say. God loves and appreciates every single utterance of praise and conversation we say to Him. It doesn't matter how long or important it may or may not be. It's the sincerity in which it's delivered is what I think God is hoping for. Aren't we all?

Please stay in touch with God on a heart to heart basis. That's all He asks for. Prayer is so very, very important.

Revisited 2016

Wow. Technology has come a long way since we had that conversation! Like most things in life, change (new technology), can be good or bad depending upon the one using it. Please don't be guilty of delegating your spiritual time with God to social media or second or even third party exchanges. Please give God the undivided "face time" that He so rightly deserves. He is waiting to hear from YOU.

Today is my beautiful daughter's birthday—March 15th. Jamie is 28 years old today. It has been thirteen years since I have been able to share this special day with her. I'm sure many of you might think that as time goes by this day gets easier or Heaven forbid—even forgotten. There couldn't be anything further from the truth.

I woke up this morning very sad—dreading the trip to the cemetery. This day there will be no birthday party. No cake. No gifts. No glees of happiness or surprise. All I can do now is take Jamie some beautiful flowers with a hand written card and lay them on her grave. My fingers will trace over each letter of her name and birth date on her marker. I **cannot** touch the space that bears the date of her death. As irrational as it sounds, it would somehow give validity to her death. I cannot do that.

It's a Monday. Jamie was born on a Monday. It is misty, dreary and overcast; much like the day she was born. The Lord has already given me gifts of comfort this morning to sustain me. Silly to some—everything to me. A song plays on the radio that was popular 14 years ago when Jamie and her brother were still at home. I am magically transported in my mind back to that place and time 14 years ago for a brief moment. I can smile and even laugh because of the wonderful memory of that time. Thank you Lord for the gift of memory. Last night I had a dream with Jamie in it. She was very young. I got to hold her and put my big, long, heavy black coat around her to keep her warm.

The day is early yet and I am longing for it to be over. For whatever reason this birthday will be a hard one for me. I cannot stop the tears. I don't know why some are harder than others. It's weird that way. The only thing I know for sure is that it wouldn't matter if I had the answer as to why, because it wouldn't change how I feel. Please pray for me, Jack and Shane today. We will need it.

One last thing, hug and kiss your children—**now**. Tell them you love them—**a lot**. I don't care how old they are. Call them on the phone if you cannot physically be with them. Don't miss your chance. **Please.**

Tonight when you sit down to eat with your children (I don't care if it's "take out" or macaroni and cheese) use the *good china*. Please don't save it for some "special" occasion—because dear friend, **you are living it**.

P.S. I must tell you this. Later today the sun broke through the clouds and poured out it's glorious warmth upon me. It was as if God was saying, "Gail, I didn't forget Jamie's birthday—or you. We're starting the party right now." I'm sure it was wonderful. I wish I could have been there. Someday I will.

Revisited 2016

With the arrival of our three youngest grandchildren, Jonah, 8 years old, and Evy and Riley, 6 year old twins, Jamie's birthday has taken on a whole new dimension for me. Three years ago Jonah, Evy and Riley wholeheartedly embraced the idea of having a birthday party for their Aunt Jamie. So now on Jamie's birthday we all go out to dinner. We put her photograph in the middle of the table. Jonah, Evy and Riley bring her beautiful fresh cut flowers and of course their birthday cards to her. We have a beautiful cake adorned with her name on it or cupcakes. And candles. Lots of candles!! We sing Happy Birthday to her and then we all blow out the candles together! It is wonderful! It is our new family tradition and hugely important to us all. This event always brings to mind the scripture where Jesus says, "Come to me as little children." I look at these three sweet faces filled with innocence and optimism. They are confident that Jamie is fine and that someday they will get to meet her in person. They have no fear or doubts. I am so proud of them.

Wouldn't the world be so much better if we could just learn to be more like them? Or more accurately—**RELEARN.**

Have you seen joy lately? No, I'm not talking about a person or a bottle of dishwashing soap. I am talking about the simple, pure, unadulterated *feeling* of joy. In my opinion it is as important to your life as is sleep, food or water. Maybe even more so. I really mean that.

I lived without joy for many years after my daughter's death. Partly because of overwhelming grief and partly because I couldn't recognize it anymore when it arrived or felt that I deserved it when it did. That being said, and by the grace of God, I now look for joy on a daily basis.

Observation tells me that many of us regard joy as some far reaching, hard to find, only for the rich commodity. It is simply not so. So why does joy seem so elusive? Maybe it's not. Maybe we have just set the bar a little too high or in the wrong places to attain it.

So what is joy anyway? Joy is the smile on your child's face—or the memory of it. It is a warm, delicious chocolate chip cookie. It is a hot, flavorful cup of coffee. It is a familiar smell that conjures up a wonderful childhood memory. It is the sound of a bird singing. It is a hug or a kiss. It is the sound of laughter. It is a job well done. It is being on the receiving end of a "Thank You." For my husband, it is cleaning his golf clubs. Now please don't think I'm talking nonsense or trivializing the subject. Please hear me out. Joy can be and is everyday things that we often take for granted until we lose it. We make finding joy much harder than it has to be.

My mother is rapidly losing her vision to a disease called macular degeneration. Through her suffering and her loss I have come to recognize the joy of being able to see everyday life that she has now lost. Fighting to maintain her independence with this disability is a joy that she is trying desperately to hang on to. Yes, independence is a joy. I am trying to open up doors of joy for her in different ways now. We **must** and we **will** find it. When we learn to recognize joy in the simplest of things then somehow in some small way we can take control of our well-being.

Some days joy seems to fall right into our laps. Other days it is nowhere to be found. On those days we have to go into the "kitchen" of our mind and whip up a batch. The recipe is simple.

(1) Bring to mind all your blessings; past and present.
(2) Mix in hope for the future.
(3) Let God stir the pot.

In no time at all your hungry soul will be fed.

One last thing—always remember that as the saying goes, "Beauty is in the eye of the beholder," so is joy. God bless you always.

Revisited 2016

J oy is hydration for the soul. Let me repeat that because this is so important! Joy is hydration for the soul. Unfortunately the signs of **dehydration** never actually manifest themselves into symptoms until we are completely or almost depleted. We don't *feel* thirsty but in reality our body is shutting down because of a lack of water (hydration). Fatigue is usually one of the very first signs one will notice when they are dehydrated. Have you ever seen a plant or flowers that had been starved of water and then received a big dose of it? Amazing how they perk up!! Their wilted blooms and leaves suddenly lift themselves up and come to life again. Their roots become anchored in the soil so they can withstand the elements.

Joy is exactly what is needed for the soul. It hydrates your soul, mind and spirit. Please do not trivialize the importance of it. Without it, the mind will deteriorate and perish. Please feed your soul daily. Look for it. Embrace it. Joy is a necessary nutrient. Drink up!

It's not often that you get a chance to go back and visit a place in your past. This experience can be exuberantly wonderful or hauntingly horrific. Yesterday I had that chance—to go and visit a place in my past. I am sad to tell you that my experience was the latter of the two—hauntingly horrific.

Many times in recent years I am called on to counsel with parents that have lost their children. God has placed this burden on my heart and I know it is the job that He has intended for me to do for the rest of my life. It is certainly not the job I wanted but it is the job given to me by God and I will do everything I can to honor Him and to help people like me. *But yesterday was different.*

Yesterday I was called to a home at the mother's request. I was particularly anxious and nervous about this visit. I knew of their son's death. Their 17 year old son had been carjacked, brutally beaten, drugged and shot execution style only two months earlier. As I expected and soon confirmed; her pain, anger, anguish and anxiety were off the charts. I visited with her for three hours.

I listened to her every word and observed her body language and every movement. I looked at her tear soaked face and pain-filled eyes that you could tell were still searching for someone to tell her that what she was living was only a dream—a horrible nightmare. I could not. She asked me tough questions with heartbreaking answers. She wanted me to take her to where my beautiful daughter, Jamie, was buried and then to where her son was buried. I did. The sadness was overwhelming and very familiar. When I came back home I wept and I wept and I wept. Partly for her and partly for me.

You see, yesterday I got a glimpse of myself many years ago. I saw a part of my past that terrified me. This mother was "me" made over. I felt as if the door to Hell had been opened again and I was terrified of falling in. I was reminded of my imprisonment there for many years. The terror of that time has left me trembling.

Please excuse me now for it is imperative that I write a "thank you" note to someone right away.

Dear God,

I inadvertently had the opportunity to visit my old neighborhood yesterday. You know the one—the one you rescued me from. Hell. It was my first visit back and I pray my last. It's hard to imagine that I could have temporarily forgotten how horrible that place was. Maybe it was a good thing that I saw it again briefly because I feel so passionate about closing that place down. I so much want to keep people from moving there. Please help me to do that, Lord.

Thank you, Lord, for rescuing me. Thank you. Thank you. Thank you. Thank you for a second chance at life. I know I will always be on the devil's "mailing list" because I am so vulnerable. But thank you Lord, for giving me the strength to recognize his literature for what it is—junk mail. I don't **EVER** want to go back. I love you.

Gail

About two years ago I finally, finally got to meet my mom. It was **so** wonderful! I've "known" her for fifty years but had never truly "met" her until recently. I promise you, there is a difference. I know that sounds weird but let me try and explain. My mother worked very hard taking care of me, my brother, my sister and dad and I appreciated that. She always had a hot meal on the table, took care of the household, made my clothes, paid the bills—all sorts of things. But it was always very difficult for her to show affection. To be perfectly honest, there were times growing up when I was even a little bit afraid of her. My dad, on the other hand, was exactly the opposite. You couldn't be in his presence without getting a "bear hug," a kiss and an "I love you." I adored him. He always made me feel special. One of the highest compliments I can pay him is the fact that he made each one of his children feel like they were his *favorite*. I don't know how he pulled it off, but he did; and there was never any jealously between us kids. **He** was the nurturer.

My father fell ill with cancer in April of 1993 and passed away in May of 1994. For 13 months I watched in amazement as my mother took care of my father. She tended his every need with the greatest of care and let him continue to "be a man" to the very end. The patience, love and respect she showed him was totally unexpected and I watched in awe. Who *was* this woman? I grew to respect her greatly. I wanted to know her. I wanted "in." I wanted to thank her for taking care of my dad—her husband. But the time still had not come as I watched her struggle after losing my dad. She is extremely independent, strong willed and definitely not a whiner. I admire these qualities.

A few years ago as I watched her health begin to decline I tried once again to "get in." Guess what? She opened the door! Not all the way at first but I could definitely see her shadow behind the door. As time went by she invited me "in." I am so happy to have finally found this wonderful friend that I wanted my whole life—and her name is MaMa. She is kind and caring and loves me very much; and I her.

I know that showing affection is very difficult for a lot of people. I, on the other hand, am just like my dad. A hug, a kiss an "I love you" is as natural as breathing to me. But it doesn't mean that my capacity for love is greater than someone who has difficulty showing affection. Absolutely not. But I plead with you; pass your love on. Please understand, I am not saying that every time you see someone you love or care about that you have to be physically affectionate. I'm talking about just a touch on the arm, a smile, whatever you feel strong enough to do. I'm sure it will be difficult at first but the rewards you will receive will calm your fears. If rejection is what you fear, I think you will find it unfounded. The blessings you will receive back will definitely be worth the risk. I am excited for you.

My mother now squeezes me tightly when I hug her. She tells me she loves me without me saying it first. I can't tell you how much this means to me. I will miss her greatly when she leaves this earth but I thank the Lord with all my heart that I got to "meet" her before she did. Please don't miss your chance. I promise you, **regret** is a terrible thing to live with.

Revisited 2016

My mother went to Heaven on Sept. 6, 2008. I miss her very much. I am so very, very thankful we didn't miss our chance to find each other before her departure.

My heart is very heavy this week for a very good friend. In four days it will be the one year anniversary of her daughter's death. Her daughter was young, beautiful and her mother's best friend for twenty-five years. This beautiful young woman did not survive a tragic automobile accident.

I know my friend is wondering in disbelief how she could possibly have breathed and existed for 365 days without her daughter being with her. How could it be possible? My heart breaks for her. She will think surely another year cannot pass again without her daughter. It just can't. She can't go on another year. But it does; and she will. She has no choice.

Perhaps on that anniversary date her eyes will look at the clock many times waiting for that awful time listed as "time of death" to come and go. Perhaps she will think of the verse in the Bible where Jesus is on the cross and says, "It is finished" as He slips into death and the clock on her wall ticks past that dreaded moment. The exhaustion she will feel is like none other; totally consuming and overwhelming. The anxiousness of this day has taken what little energy she has left. The past year she has been forced to endure her birthday, her daughter's birthday, Mother's Day, Thanksgiving and Christmas without her beautiful daughter. And now the final insult—the anniversary date of her daughter's death. She wants everyone to remember what day this is; but to be left alone at the same time. Everything stings so badly. I wish I could take her pain away; but I can't. It simply cannot be avoided or shifted to someone else. There is so much for her to learn; to sort out. It is excruciating.

I am praying desperately for my friend. I know God's mercy will be her life preserver. It already has. She has been *afloat* for a year now—treading water. I pray she will not drown. She doesn't have to. But sometimes the anger, confusion, sadness and fatigue weight you down; keep you flailing in the water. I know this.

Please, dear friend, don't give up. Your daughter doesn't want that. She loves you very much. Carry your daughter's love and legacy on until you get to be with her again. Believe me, I know it is horribly hard to do. But God will hold onto you and give you gifts of your daughter to sustain you if you will let Him. Please let Him.

In four days my friend will need our prayers. Please, please pray for my friend. Thank you.

A ugust. Just another month, right? Not for me. Each year about the end of July, I begin to panic. My mind starts retracing the events of an awful August day in 1991. August 27th to be exact. On that day I lost my best friend. My confidante. My make-up artist. My wardrobe planner. My cheerleader in Life. My beautiful teenage daughter, Jamie. My mind will start down a path I know to be dangerous, but I cannot help myself. My memory will transport me back to the beginning of August 1991. I will vividly recall the events of each day leading up to her accident. The anticipation of school starting. Shopping trips to the mall with her to buy school clothes; what fun! The photo session at the High School for the football programs. She was on the Pom Pon Squad. The trip we took to Lackland Air Force Base in San Antonio to see her brother, Shane, not knowing it would be her last. The night before her accident—she lying in her bed and me in mine, talking across the hall to each other—laughing as we drifted off to sleep. Our final good-bye that morning. A kiss, a hug, an "I love you." Taking for granted the words, "I'll see you this evening" to be true. Why not? Why should *this* day be any different? The car crash. The Fire Chief at my front door.

Thirteen years later, I still wonder how I could have stopped it from happening. The devil will take advantage of my timely weakness and attack me with everything he's got. Some years I lose. Some years it engulfs me. Swallows me. Consumes me. I can *feel* myself being sucked down the drain. I hate those years. I know God's hand is reaching out to catch me but some years I am just too tired to grab hold. That is when God picks me up and carries me. Thank you Lord for your mercy.

Please God, let it be September.

So…Here it is July 31st and I can hardly wait to turn the calendar to August. "What?" you ask. "Have I suddenly found closure? Am I healed?" The answer is "No" and "No."

In one month, on August 31st, the act of an enormously kind, caring man will make a dream come true for me and my husband, Jack. We have never met this man but because of his compassion, we will on August 31st. He is fulfilling a life long dream of my husband; to actually *meet* the person he admires most. This man is giving him the generosity of his time—of himself. I don't know if this man fully recognizes the magnitude of his gift; but I suspect he will when he meets my husband and me. We are **beyond** excited!

You see, this man is very talented and because of that talent he has many obligations that pull him in many different directions. He is a professional. He is a businessman. He is a father; a husband. I am sure he is many, many wonderful things to many people. But to Gail Bennett Fry, he is an answer to prayer. Nothing short of a miracle.

Thank you, Mr. Jack Nicklaus for your kindness; for your response; for your caring. Thank you. Thank you. Thank you.

Thank you, Mrs. Nicklaus, Marilyn Keough and Scott Tolley, for your part in making this happen. Thank you. Thank you. Thank you.

August will always be a very difficult month for me but because of one man's extraordinary kindness it will forever hold a glimpse of happiness.

Happy Birthday, Jack.

I love words. The dictionary is my second favorite book—only beat out by the Bible. I keep my dictionary close at hand so I can look up any word that is new to me. Election years are great! Politicians are a huge source of new words. Every two to four years we are introduced to new words through political strategies. Words like moot, pundit, debacle and so on. I have also learned that there is a huge difference between knowing the definition of a word and experiencing the true meaning of it. I had always known the definition of the word "sob" but never experienced the true meaning of it until I lost my daughter, Jamie. To "sob" is **so** much more than the normal act of crying. Sobbing is an uncontrollable, involuntary, gut wrenching, body shaking, wailing experience. I remember there were many times that I would put my first two fingers horizontally inside my mouth and bite down on them so my upper and lower teeth would not bang against each other. I have also experienced the meaning of words like despair, anger, depression, hopelessness. And now, years later and by the grace of God, I am learning the meaning of words like joy, hopeful, perseverance, peace.

I was very blessed to witness the true meaning of the word "faith" just weeks before Jamie's accident. Jamie and I had driven into a neighborhood where her dad and I were looking at a piece of property to build a house on. It was truly out of our price range but we were looking anyway. Jamie was **so** excited! Here was her chance to get a two story house. (All girls love two story houses.) We got back in the car and were driving off when I turned to her and realistically said, "Honey, we can't build a house here. It's just too expensive. We can't afford it." She looked at me in utter amazement and defiantly said, "Yes, we can. Daddy said so." I almost laughed out loud until I looked into her face and saw what Jesus must have seen when He encountered the centurion on the road. This was the face of the centurion. This was what the "face of faith" looked like.

You see, in Jamie's eyes, heart and mind anything her daddy said to her was true. She believed in him. She had total faith in him and his ability and was amazed and maybe even a little bit angry that I didn't.

I am so thankful the Lord let me see first hand what the "face of faith" looks like. I pray daily that I can be that "face of faith" for someone, everyone. I will be so happy when I am with Jamie again and can tell her all of my experiences. I have complete and utter faith that I will be with her again. And you want to know **WHY** I am so sure of that? It is because my "Daddy (my Heavenly Father) said so." Thank you, Lord.

I **LOVE** to watch detective shows—*Law and Order*, all of the *CSI's* and especially a new one called *The Closer* starring Kyra Sedgwick. I try earnestly to figure out who the "bad guy" is and I love to be challenged by the script. Jack and I spend almost the entire hour trying to figure it out. It forces you to listen and look for the smallest of details and I definitely think that's good for the 'ol brain.

Last night when I was watching one of these programs I had a wonderful revelation that startled me just a little bit. All of these shows always start off with at least one, if not more, murders or horrible attacks of some kind. You know—to set the scenario for the show. The one I was watching was particularly violent in nature. This poor woman had been beaten, raped, limbs amputated, set on fire and thrown into a lake. Can't get much worse than that. I was sitting there thinking how horrible this would be if it was happening to me. And then my next thought was, that no matter what the outcome, I would be safe. And then I thought, **"WHAT?!"** (I talk to myself a lot, by the way.) But an overwhelming sense of peace came over me right there in my living room sitting on my couch. It was true. I would be safe even if those horrible things happened to me and took my life. I would be safe because I am saved. I felt an enormous relief and reassurance.

Now I'll be the first to tell you that I am not looking forward to dying—but I'm not afraid of it either. You see; I have reservations. When I leave this world I already have a place secured for me—Heaven. That gives me the confidence to not be afraid of death—only afraid of the physical pain that may accompany it. That's human nature. Yes, I am a sissy when it comes to physical pain and violence. I hope to avoid it like the plague when it comes my time to die. I hope to go peacefully in my sleep—but that may not be the case. I have no control over that. But the one and most important thing I **do** have control over is my destination after this life. God gives us free choice and Jesus gives us a chance. I hope and pray that you will take advantage of the gift of eternal life while you still can if you haven't already. It truly gives meaning to the words "peace that passeth understanding." Please don't wait—because death doesn't.

I adore my dad. I think I told you that before. He was the kind of person that leapt at the chance to help someone else and then made you feel like **you** had done **him** a favor. He made you feel good about yourself. He was very observant and always generous with compliments or words of encouragement—whichever was needed. He was genuine and kind. He was very intelligent and held a high ranking job but always made you feel like he was a "regular guy." To know him was to love him. I **never, ever** wanted to disappoint him. He taught me many, many things throughout my life but one of the most valuable lessons he taught me was how important it is to "do the right thing" even when you thought no one else was watching. I learned about honor, honesty and integrity at a very young age. My father left me with these words of wisdom that he repeated many times to me all throughout my life. I think of these words almost daily. They are definitely worth repeating. Please listen closely.

My father would say to me, "Gail, be careful how you live your life. You never know, YOU may be the only

Bible some people will ever read." Wow. How true. Our lives are an open book for anyone to read. Anyone who happens to glance in our direction can read a paragraph about us without us even realizing it. The responsibility is awesome but not heavy if we know God.

My father never compromised his values or his beliefs. His life was a "very good book" and read by many, many people. I know he made a difference—a positive one. We can too. God bless you always.

Gail

I believe there is one word spoken in any language that every person on this planet longs for and strives to be. It's a very simple sounding word that is seen, heard and spoken everywhere, everyday and ohhh—so taken for granted. Most of us are completely satisfied with just the basic fulfillment of this word while there is a certain percentage of those who find it only acceptable if it has the prefix "above" before it. And perhaps we all struggle with the fear that the prefix "ab" or "below" may suddenly appear without warning when describing ourselves. Have you figured out what it is yet? Yes, you're right. The word is **normal**. It is truly "the measuring stick of the world."

We somehow associate "normal" as supreme wellness, powerful, intelligent, in control. I think we will all agree that it certainly gives us a sense of calm.

Now please stay with me. I'm about to let you in on a little secret about myself that only a handful of people know. I am terrified to expose this about myself. I have tried desperately for so long to conceal it, but if my revelation can help even one person, then it will be worth it. Now there are three things about myself that I will never tell you—my weight, my cholesterol level and my I.Q. Mainly because I do not **know** any of these numbers and do not care to know. I figure, "Hey! Why ruin a perfectly good day!" All other information about me is up for grabs! Poor Jack.

What I suffer with is Obsessive Compulsive Disorder (OCD for short) and when I say "suffer" I don't mean that lightly. It is a terribly frustrating, embarrassing, debilitating disorder that many, many people suffer with daily. And **NO**—It is not contagious. You don't have to put the book down. (That would be an OCD thought.) For those of you unfamiliar with this disorder I will try to enlighten you a little bit. It goes well **beyond quirkiness**. It is a feeling of "impending doom" that follows you in most everything you do. It causes people to repeat their actions or thoughts over and over again—such as hand washing, checking knobs on stoves to make sure they're turned off, locks on doors, all sorts of things. It's a feeling as if you can't trust your own eyes to believe what you see. It makes simple everyday tasks hardships in many cases because it becomes so time consuming. Believe me, nobody *wants* to be like this. More often than not, people with OCD are perfectionists. So you can only imagine how this makes the affliction even more challenging. I could go on and on with many examples of OCD behavior-each one more baffling and bizarre than the next. And just when you think you have conquered one OCD habit a new one suddenly appears out of nowhere to take its place. I recently heard Howard Hughes being described as a "victim" of OCD. I thought that was a very good way of putting it. *Victim*—Fighting an invisible enemy. The only face it wears is the one whose reflection stares back at you in the mirror. Maddening? You betcha!

Not only is it very hard for the people affected with this disorder; it is also very difficult for the people who live with and love them. My wonderful husband, Jack, has watched me suffer with this for most of our married life. He doesn't have it so he certainly can't understand it. (Heck, **I** don't understand it!) But he patiently watches me—never criticizing or persecuting me. I am painfully aware of this. I promise you—if there was a winning lottery ticket sitting inside my head, Jack would not go in to get it. Yes, it's **that** scary! I am pretty good at hiding it in public and when I am totally engrossed in something (like social situations) thankfully it doesn't surface as often or as intense. It's very strange indeed.

Okay. Now you know this about me. Does it change how you feel about me? Am I still normal to you? Do you still like me? You see, to some, in the eyes of the world I would be considered broken, worthless, less than perfect—**not normal.** Some would simply choose to throw me away. How sad.

Yes, I have an affliction that I wish I didn't have; but I will **not** let it defeat me. I will just try harder, start things earlier and plan to stay later—but I will not give up. Someday the Lord may heal me from this affliction but if He doesn't, that's okay, because I know He will give me the extra strength and courage to endure. I believe that.

For me—normal has got to be a "state of mind" not a "state of being." Or better yet, maybe we can all agree that normal is a "state of the heart." That way God is the judge; not man.

School started today; Wednesday, Aug. 17th. Fourteen years ago August 17th was on a Saturday. I remember it vividly. Jamie jumped out of bed early to get ready for the day. Today was picture day at the High School. School was starting the next week. They were taking pictures today for the High School Football program. Pictures of the football players, cheerleaders, pom pon girls, coaches. She put on her uniform, grabbed her pom pons and raced out the door. A whole new life ahead of her and she wasn't going to miss any of it. Later that day we went shopping for school clothes and we actually **agreed** on many clothing items! Can you believe it?! She had a certain amount of money to spend and she was **so** careful to make it go as far as possible. She was a much better money manager than me and certainly more self disciplined when it came to money. No impulse buys for this girl! Her joy, happiness, anticipation for life was contagious. She infected us all. Ten days later, without any warning, she was gone. You know the rest…

I think about this day, Aug. 17th, and the events that followed every day of my life. What I want to talk to you about always surfaces at this time of year (school starting) with such intensity and conviction that I no longer can hold back. I believe that what I am about to tell you is **THE** most important thing that I, or anyone else, can tell you.

MAKE SURE YOUR KIDS ARE SAVED.

Now please, before you stop listening and tell me that your kids go to church every Sunday or they were christened as a child so you have it all covered—please, please hear me out. I will be brief, I promise.

You and I both know, as adults, that there is a big difference between *knowing* about God (which everybody does) and being saved. I *know* about a lot of celebrities but I don't have a personal relationship with them. Being saved is having a personal relationship with God—not just having knowledge of His existence. Make **sure** your kids know the difference. Talk to them. Dig deep. Make sure. Please don't put this off. Remember when I told you a moment ago that Jamie left without warning? Well, that's usually how it happens. I know we all believe that terrible things will never happen to us or any of our kids. It always happens to "Somebody Else"—not us. Well, let me introduce myself to you. **I am "Somebody Else."** And guess what? I look like you. I think like you. I work hard like you. I enjoy things like you. I love my kids like you. **I could be you.**

When Jamie and her brother were still living home, every time they would get ready to go somewhere I would give them my "MOM" speech. You know the one—"Wear your seat belt"; "Call me when you get there"; "Don't drive too fast"—all the warning signals. When they no longer seemed to pay attention to that particular speech, I came up with a new one. Same warnings, new ending. After I gave them my "speech" I looked at them and without flinching a muscle I said, "I can't help you when you're dead." It stopped them cold. "What?!" they asked. "Wow!" I thought. " I got their attention!" **Now** they would listen to my warnings. Never in a hundred million years did I ever think that I would live to know the meaning of those words. They haunt me to this day. But you know what? I was right and I didn't want to be. I only said them to get their attention. There is not a single thing I can do for Jamie now. Nothing. All I can do is put some flowers in a vase and clean a marker with her name on it. But because I knew Jamie was saved I know our separation is only temporary. And I promise you, when they are gone that is the only thing that will matter. Will I be with them again? Were they saved? And it is the **ONLY** thing you cannot fix or change. Please, dear friend, don't put off the most important thing in your and your child's life. The separation is hard enough knowing it's only temporary—unbearable knowing it's not.

ι are getting your kids ready for school
ιentally going over the check list of all the
.eed to take to school with them—**please,**
forget the most important thing. Make sure
;od in their heart. You will never be sorry.

Gail

Fear is a funny thing. It can lie dormant for many years and then suddenly rise up within you and strike as viciously and venomously as a rattlesnake. Its poison races quickly through your body and can leave you ravaged or worse if not treated quickly. There is only one antidote—faith and trust in God. That being said, I have to tell you of a great fear that is looming on the horizon for me as we speak.

This year, 2006, will mark a passage of time that scares me to death. This year I will enter the "time zone" where I will have lived longer on this earth without Jamie than with her. It grips my heart. I have thought about this for a very long time and the closer it gets the more anxious I feel. I don't know why exactly or what particular difference it will make but the thought of it just makes me very, very sad. Recently I had a conversation with a friend who lost her teenage son the same year we lost Jamie. During our conversation she verbalized to me the very same fear that I was already preparing myself for. Their son was 19 years old when he died. They have four more years before this "time zone" will become reality for them. I, on the other hand, have run out of time. It will come no matter what I do to try and stop it. Maybe when it passes I will be able to help my friend. Four years goes by so quickly.

I believe that information is vital to survival. I think that's why I talk to you so much. I just want to make sure you know that the thoughts and feelings you have are not unlike mine or many others. I just want to make sure you know you are **NOT** going crazy. And for me, any validation of saneness is a welcome visitor in my crowded thoughts.

I know the devil has marked this date on his calendar—August 2006—*Devour Gail. Finish her off.* But that will not happen. I have been warned. I know God will give me the strength I need. He will sustain me.

Maybe it won't be as bad as I think. Still…it worries me. Please pray for me. I'll get back to you.

Gail

Fear—False Evidence Appearing Real
SO TRUE.

Revisited 2016

I don't know what to say. In Five Months it will be 25 years since Jamie's accident. 25 years without her. Unbelievable. I am very, very sad. Not afraid. Just sad.

Dear Friend,

Thank you so much for sharing your time with me. It is truly a blessing for me as I pray it is for you. I would like to close our time together with a letter to Jamie. I miss talking to her *so* much. I take every chance I get. Thanks.

One last thing I am compelled to tell you. Please know that the Lord loves you so very, very much. He is so eager to help you with whatever situation you may find yourself in; no matter how bleak, horrible or hopeless it may seem. I know this to be true because **I am living proof.**

Until next time,
Gail

"Yet the Lord longs to be gracious to you; he rises to show you compassion. For the Lord is a God of justice. Blessed are all who wait for him!" (Isaiah 30:18)

Hi Jamie,

It's MaMa. I just thought I'd drop you a line and let you know how we're doing. Yes, I *still* write letters the old fashioned way—with an ink pen, stationery and stamps. **I know, I know;** E-Mail is much faster and easier but remember how technologically challenged I was? Still am. Absolutely no improvement whatsoever. We actually **do** have a computer but I couldn't turn it on if my life depended on it! I'm still waiting for the "Star Trek" version to come out. You know—the one where you just sit down and **talk** to it! Then watch out! I'll be flying down the internet highway! Yeah, right! Anyway, for now I just pray the U.S. Post Office stays in business!

It's hard to believe that you are 28 years old. I know you are still beautiful; just like I last saw you. I often try to envision what you look like at 28. I see your school friends and how they have matured and I wonder... I'm sure you still have your long hair—that's a given. Your beautiful smile (without the braces!) and twinkling green eyes I'm sure are just as mesmerizing. I watch our home videos and listen to tapes of you just to make sure I don't ever forget the sound of your voice; your laughter. I would give anything to feel your touch again. I study your handwriting to make sure I will always be able to recognize it. Many of your school friends have children of their own now. I am so, so sorry that you missed out on that blessing. I know for a fact that you would have been the "cool" mom. You know—the one all the kids like and want to be around. Comfortable. Laid back. Cool. I am sure God has you very busy using those talents helping young children who are temporarily without their earthly parents. He wouldn't let all your love go to waste. I am so proud of you.

I dream of you often. What's strange, is that in my dreams you are almost always very young—about 2 to 8 years old. I don't know why that is but I am just so thankful for them. I get to be "your mom" again. Do things for you; take care of you. I miss that so much. Many times now I feel like *you* are taking care of me. Strange, huh?

The other day your dad played a *Dire Straits* CD while we were in his truck together. I know you and Shane played that same CD a million times before at home and it all sounded wonderfully familiar to me except for one song—an instrumental. It was absolutely beautiful! All I could think about after that was, "Did Jamie hear this song? She must have. I can't **believe** we didn't 'discuss' this song." It made me sad to realize that there were so many questions that I would have asked you if I had only known you were going away. As close as we were, there was so much more I **needed, wanted** to know. But I know with all of my heart that the Lord blessed me by not letting me know ahead of time that you were leaving. I would have ruined our last days together by worry, trying to change things, being over protective. As it was, our last days together were just like the previous 15 years—**Glorious.**

As time goes by, the devil is always on the prowl trying to convince me that all our happiness together was somehow a figment of my imagination. Rob me of my security. I have to stand strong against him. I know he wants to destroy me. The Lord is so wonderful! He steps in during those moments and gives me gifts of confirmation—a wonderful picture of us together; a new memory that has been in storage in my brain; a testimony from a friend or relative reliving a time with you. God is very creative. Thank you Lord for your mercy.

You won't believe what I'm about to tell you next! I wrote a book. Two of them!! Can you believe it?! **I know, I know;** I'm the girl who said the thought of "curling up with a good book" was about as appealing as plucking my eyebrows. I remember. To be honest, I still don't read anything but newspapers and magazines. As you know, I'm not a very patient person. But for whatever reason, the Lord has placed this enormous burden for me to write down my thoughts. Weird, huh? And get this—I actually am enjoying it. It helps me to write down what I'm feeling. It's kind of like letting out this secret that you've been holding forever; bursting to let go of. I pray that my thoughts are helping people. That is certainly their intent. I am just trying to do what God tells me to do. I have to.

Your dad and Shane are doing well. In fact, today is your dad's birthday. He is on duty at the Fire Station. You **won't believe** the wonderful gift the Lord blessed us with for your dad's birthday! He got to personally **meet** Jack Nicklaus! (I will always believe you had a hand in this.) Isn't that cool?! Someday I'll show you all the pictures. It was fantastic!!

In about two months Shane will be moving to Florida. He's still in the Air Force. He has been in for 13 years. Incredible! I am so proud of him. I know you two love each other so much. I know the pain Shane feels will never go away; just like for all of us. I say never—it will when we are all together again. We know that. You would be so proud of him. He is married to a wonderful girl named Brittney. He also has a beautiful little girl named MeKayela. I **know** you'll love them! Shane is trustworthy, responsible, compassionate and a very hard worker. I am so blessed.

Well Jamie, I can hardly bring myself to talk to you about this but I know I must. It probably will seem silly to some but certainly not to you and me. Jamie, when you left, Cookie was only 2 years old. At the time I thought, "What am I going to do with Jamie's dog?" I knew immediately I would always take care of her for you. And you know me—I'm not the *animal lover* that you are. Boy! That sounds awful, doesn't it? I mean I love animals—I just don't want the responsibility of caring for them. That was your job and you loved it. Well, without much coaxing, I fell totally in love with your dog. Taking care of her went from being a responsibility to being a blessing. She watched over me just like she did with you. She listened to my late night cries and tried her best to comfort me. She brought so much joy to me and asked for nothing in return. All she wanted was for me to love her; which I so very much did. I tried my very best to take good care of her. Cookie got sick and we did everything we could to get her well. But on April 26th, in the last moments of her life, I held her body close to mine. She drew her final breath and I could *feel* her slip from my arms into yours. She's back home with you, sweet baby. Back home with you. I am weeping as we speak. She was 15 years old when she left this earth, just like you. Take good care of her, baby. I know you will.

Well sweetheart, I must close for now and go wash my face. I have **GOT** to start using waterproof mascara! This stuff burns my eyes so bad not to mention the mess it makes on my face!!

I love you Jamie, with all my heart. What a glorious day it will be when we are all together again! But you want to know what's hard? **The wait.** The wait is so very,

very hard. But I promise you I won't let you down. I will try my best to help others and make my life meaningful. I will wear your smile. And when I fall down (and I will) I will use your energy to get back up. God will sustain me. I trust Him.

My dear, dear Jamie—I love you, love you, love you.
Mom

Revisited

2016

You wouldn't think something that happened 25 years ago could still bring you to your knees, would you? You would be wrong. In the last month our family once again suffered another untimely and sudden tragedy with the death of a teenage boy who is a son, a brother, a grandson, a nephew, a cousin, a friend. He is handsome, smart, articulate and fun. He is Brenner. I love the mother and father of this young man very much and they have always held a very special place in my heart. In the days following the news of his death, I watched in horror the pain, suffering, anguish and confusion that has been so vividly displayed on their faces and tortured bodies—all without their knowledge. It has been gut wrenching and heart breaking to watch. A few years after losing Jamie I had a family member tell me that I looked like someone had taken a baseball bat and beat me up one side and down the other. At the time she disclosed that to me I was puzzled by her words. Now I understood. I was now witnessing what she had seen in me. Watching this mom and dad was like watching a movie I had seen 25 years ago. **WAY** too familiar. I played a leading role in that movie. I didn't audition for the part but got it anyway. I didn't *want* the role or any part of this film. It debuted August 27,1991 much to my protest. It is a horror film. It is scarier than any knife wielding monster you could imagine. You cannot run away from the pain being inflicted because you can't see it coming. The movie starts out with a man and woman, also known as mom and dad, being told that their worst nightmare has been realized. Your child has been killed, your child has died, your child is dead. The plot that unfolds is the daily pain and misery that ensues. I want to get out of this theatre and run away as fast as I can! I can't close my eyes and make it go away because the scenes are etched into my memory, my mind's eye. I cannot make it stop. It will have to play out.

I am on my knees.

W ords of comfort. They don't exist. **Sorry.** When you lose a child you are inconsolable. I know you want to say or do something to ease the horrible sorrow you see before you, but sadly, you cannot. I have fallen victim to this many times myself.

However, there **are** some things that many people tend to say in these situations that only bring additional pain and frustration. Here are a few.

PLEASE don't say, "Well, they are in a better place now." **I KNOW THAT.** But that does not ease my pain, sorrow and longing to be with them.

"I know just how you feel," said by an individual that has never lost a child. Sorry, but you do **NOT** know how I feel and please be thankful that you don't.

And then I have heard many people say, " Everything happens for a reason." **No it doesn't.** God's plan is altered every day by mankind. God can certainly take a horrible tragedy and use it to bring about something positive but please don't say these words to a bereaved parent. It does **not** help.

Fact is, there is absolutely nothing to say beyond, "I am so sorry. Is there anything I can do? I love you. I am praying for you." That's it.

The **only** words of consolation for me after losing Jamie would have been the following, "Oh, Gail, there has been a terrible mistake! Jamie isn't gone after all! She's right in the next room waiting for you!" **THOSE** would have been comforting words. Sadly, no one could speak them to me.

Please forgive me if I have sounded mean or ungrateful during this conversation. I know how much you want to help and that's the reason I am telling you these things. We stumble over ourselves and our words because we don't know what to do. Myself included. So please, just love and support this parent. Be there for them. And pray. Please pray. They are different people now.

I have never laid eyes on Jamie's death certificate, nor ever had possession of it. **EVER.** When asked where it was to be sent I only knew it could not come to my house. It was sent to my parent's home. I could not bear the thought of that document lying next to Jamie's birth certificate neatly in a folder disguised as being totally innocuous when in reality its content held enormous pain and suffering for me and my family. It could **not** reside with me.

In the following days, months and years after Jamie's accident I would come to learn just how much my family, friends, community and people I didn't even know would nurture me.

It's odd how we never outgrow our immediate reaction to fear or pain is to run to our parents. For safety, comfort, protection. That is **literally** what I did when told the news of Jamie's accident. I physically ran to their house and collapsed on their floor. Horrible news couldn't follow me there, right? Wrong. From that moment on my parents stepped back into their protective Mom and Dad roles and watched over me. Their child had been wounded. **Deeply.** They did everything humanly possible to help me and Jack. My mom kept Jamie's unwelcome death certificate until she died. Thank you Mom and Dad. I love you so much.

My twin brother, Dale, walked into my bedroom (where I was hiding) the day of Jamie's accident, told me he loved me and he would take care of everything. He did. During Jamie's memorial service Military jets happened to fly over and I remember hearing someone say, "I bet Dale ordered that too!" Thank you Dale. I love you so much.

My sister, Nila, took me to restaurants outside of town because I was so afraid to be around people I knew. She cloaked me with any sort of protection she could possibly think of. She now courageously holds the unwelcome document for me in MaMa's stead. Thank you Nila. I love you so much.

I know *everyone* thinks that they have the best friends on the planet—**but I really do.** My friends loved me unconditionally. They loved me in spite of my aloofness, despondency and confusion. They **never** gave up on me. They stood beside me. They waited patiently for me to come back. Thank you all. I love you all so much.

I also live in the best community in the world. My community came to our aid in prayer, acts of kindness, cards, letters, food and help in so **many** ways. Many from people I had never even met. They were wonderful. My church welcomed me back without any questions after my long and angry absence. Thank you all. I love you so much.

There is one last person I have to thank for doing a very difficult task. This is extremely difficult for me to talk about. Please bear with me. It is the Air Force Chaplain who had to deliver the agonizing news of Jamie's death to Shane—Jamie's brother, our son. Shane was in Biloxi, Mississippi on that fateful day serving our country. He was 19 years old. This was his first time away from home and he was in a place where he was totally unfamiliar, surrounded by people he didn't know. The letter the Chaplain wrote to me afterwards is so private and so painful I cannot bear to share it. Suffice it to say he told me how incredibly brave my son was in the midst of such devastating news and how very proud I should be of him. **I am dear sir, I am.** It breaks my heart that I was not there for him. Shane will always be my child and when **he hurts, I hurt.** Thank you dear Chaplain for taking care of my son in my absence. I cannot dwell on this subject any further. The cut is too deep. I fear I will bleed out. My apologies.

Each and every one of these people, collectively, cradled me in their arms and tried desperately to breathe life back into me. To them I say, **"Thank you! Thank you! Thank you! I'm back!"**

WOW. It has been quite a journey and I still have not yet reached my destination—at home with Jesus and Jamie. That has been my purpose since August 27, 1991. The strange thing is—I'm not quite as anxious to get there as when I started out. That sounds so terrible when I say that out loud, doesn't it? Believe me, the devil is whispering in my ear as we speak telling me how disloyal I am being to Jamie. The closer I get to the truth and freedom the louder his taunts will become. This guy is very good at his job. I am strong enough now to ignore his rants. Thank you Lord. So please, don't misunderstand what I'm trying to say. I am still **VERY** anxious to get to Heaven. I would just like to delay my arrival for a little while longer. Some people will immediately say that I am healed **(YUK!!)** or that my love for Jamie has dimmed. Both are so blatantly false and it breaks my heart that anyone would think that. I love and miss Jamie even more than on the day she left. My heart will be broken until I see the smile on her face and feel the touch of her embrace once again.

The Lord has blessed me so much. It is very difficult to explain how I feel now—25 years later. To put into words the life lessons that would make me feel so differently about fast forwarding my date with destiny. Perhaps Jamie can say it best for me. Please listen to her words very carefully. They are powerful, potent and liberating. I pray they will speak to you and give you relief and rest.

Always,
Gail

Dear Mom,

Hi! It's Jamie! Please don't be afraid! Remember when you used to say that God works in mysterious ways? Well, believe it! His power and wisdom is limitless and beyond comprehension. He knows exactly **when, who** and **how** to reach out when something needs to be addressed. So please, don't be afraid. **Just listen.**

First of all, I love you, Dad, Shane (and his cute family) and everybody **SO** much! I am so very proud of you too! I know it has been very tough on you and I am so proud you are still standing! Who knew that it would take such enormous faith, courage and strength just to go on? I wanted to tell you something that I hope will help you. I am writing because I want you to know that I give you permission. Permission to go on with your life and be happy doing it. I know you well enough Mom, to recognize that you need to hear those words from me. I remember your fierce loyalty to Shane and me.

But Mom, if you think that denying yourself of a full and happy life is somehow being loyal to me you are very wrong. It is quite the opposite. I know how much you love me and miss me. I know my name is always on the tip of your tongue. I appreciate and love you for that. But the gift of life is so precious! It is our responsibility to live it to the fullest. **I did.** I know you don't understand why I am not there with you but that is simply not for us to know at this time. But, oh my gosh Mom, think about how great it will be when we are all together again, in Heaven! I don't know when that time will be but until then I have work to do and so do you.

Remember when you told me that children are an extension of their parents? That I was an extension of you? Well now you are an extension of me, Mom. I know that's not how you think it's supposed to be. Certainly not how you imagined it. The natural order of life and all that stuff. **I get it.** But Mom, you represent me now more than ever.

So please, wear me proudly and with a beautiful smile. Thanks Mom. I knew I could count on you.

I know I am not forgotten and believe me, **neither are you.** Take good care of yourself, Mom, because I love you.

Your daughter,
Jamie Lin Fry

Dear Jamie,

Thank you sweet baby. Thank you.

All My Love Forever and Ever,
Mom

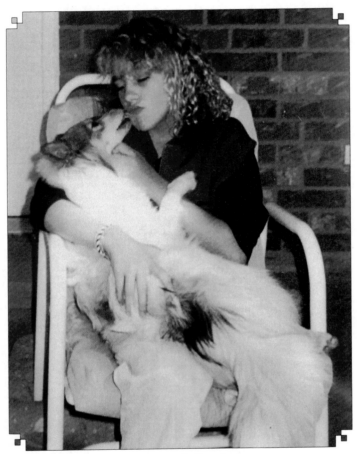

Jamie and Cookie

Jack Fry

mwcgolfer@cox.net